KATHLEEN WOODWARD, one of five children, was born in 1896 in Peckham, south London. Her father was a lithographic printer, but at the time of Kathleen's birth was working as a casual labourer in the printing trade. Whether the family moved north to Bermondsey – to the area of the imaginary Jipping Street – is not known. But at twelve, Kathleen Woodward began to work in a factory on the north side of the Thames and by the outbreak of war she was in a Bermondsey collar factory. During this period she met Mary Macarthur, then Secretary of the National Federation of Women Workers (Miss Doremus in *Jipping Street* might well be a portrait of her).

In the following years she worked her passage across the Atlantic, was a receptionist in a London club, wrote children's stories, and worked as a freelance journalist. In 1927 her first book, *Queen Mary,* was published, her interest in her no doubt fostered by Mary Macarthur's friendship with the queen. *Jipping Street* appeared in 1928, and Kathleen Woodward was fêted as 'the daughter of a washer-woman who grew up to be the biographer of a queen'. She converted to Catholicism in the 1930s, and died in 1961.

# JIPPING STREET

## KATHLEEN WOODWARD

WITH A NEW INTRODUCTION BY
CAROLYN STEEDMAN

Virago

*To*

# M.D.M.

Published by VIRAGO PRESS Limited 1983
Ely House, 37 Dover Street, London W1X 4HS

First published 1928 by Longmans, Green and Company
Copyright © The Estate of Kathleen Woodward 1961
Introduction copyright © Carolyn Steedman 1983

Virago edition offset from Longmans, Green 1928 edition

*British Library Cataloguing in Publication Data*
Woodward, Kathleen
Jipping Street.
1.  Woodward, Kathleen     2.  London (England)
—Biography
I.   Title
942.1′092′4         DA574.W1
ISBN 0-86068-390-7

Printed in Great Britain by litho at
The Anchor Press, Tiptree, Essex

The front cover shows a woodcut by John Nash from
the first edition of *Jipping Street* and a detail from 'A
Zandvoort Fishing Girl', 1884 by Elizabeth Stanhope
Forbes, reproduced by kind permission of the Newlyn
Orion Galleries, Penzance.

# CONTENTS

# INTRODUCTION

*Jipping Street* is a psychological account of growing up female and working class. It is about a mother who is not the martyred saint of traditional male working-class autobiography, whose child, Kathleen Woodward, is bound to her not by love, nor by gratitude, but by a fierce sense of resentment and debt. On a first reading, the insistent repetition of the narrative seems to speak out of a historical darkness. But, in fact, what Kathleen Woodward has to say here about the relationship of mothers and daughters in working-class households is written in many places, it is just that we have few ways as yet of reading the words that convey a similar message about the tension and despair of our first affective relationship. 'I hate my mother', said Maggie Fuller in *Dutiful Daughters,* and we are not yet in a position to understand what she meant.[1]

First published in 1928, *Jipping Street* offers an account of the author's childhood and adolescence in Bermondsey, some time before the First World War. It confirms other accounts of working-class childhood at the turn of the century, particularly of children's usefulness in 'the helping years' between starting school and going out to work.[2] The account Kathleen Woodward presents of her childhood introduction to socialism, her search for self-education through membership of socialist, suffrage and free-thought groups throws light on other autobiographical descriptions of similar political educations of the 1890s and 1900s.[3] The diffuse religiosity that came to permeate London socialist groups in the years before the First

World War is outlined here in the chapter 'Sons and Daughters of Revolt',[4] and her plain and pecuniary account of women and trade union organisation is a piece of counter evidence to more conventional records of the relationship between work and politics in this period.

So if Kathleen Woodward's book is to be read as history, then it confirms to some extent other reports of working-class life and politics in Edwardian London. But readers mining the book for historical evidence should be warned: *Jipping Street* is not what it seems, and it needs to be read as case-history rather than history. Details of time, place and politics are used by Kathleen Woodward to construct a psychological narrative rather than a historical one, and because of this, the *meaning* of events described is of a different order from that of the very same events when written about elsewhere.

Kathleen Doris Woodward was born in September 1896, in Peckham – south of the Old Kent Road, in fact, a geographical boundary that she gives to the Bermondsey she describes in *Jipping Street*. She was one of five children, and her father was a lithographic printer, a skilled man, though at the time of Kathleen's birth working as a casual labourer in the printing trade. It is not clear if the family later moved north, towards the river, into Bermondsey proper; but as Kathleen Woodward implicitly recognised when she set her childhood there, to be born in the ordinary poverty of south London's endless streets is not enough, not bad enough. The writer must move north, or east, closer to the river, to Mile End or Whitechapel, in order to place a childhood in a real slum, and make it worthy of attention.

By setting her childhood in pre-First World War Bermondsey, Kathleen Woodward recognised an almost virgin literary territory. When a philanthropic settlement was established there in the 1890s, its founder noted that it was

> at that time the most neglected neighbourhood of poorer London . . . the south side was practically off the map, derelict. It had neither the advantages nor the disadvantages of the appalling East End. It had not been written up like the Mile End Road or the Ratcliffe Highway . . .[5]

By 1911, Bermondsey had been written up, by Alexander Paterson, in *Across the Bridge*.[6] His description is echoed here; but Jipping Street never actually existed, though it was placed by Kathleen Woodward with great topographical detail upon the Bermondsey map. The closest geographical match to it is Weston Street, which at the turn of the century ran from Guy's Hospital, south to the Old Kent Road. But houses described in this book were not a feature of Weston Street, and no canal ever ran parallel to it. The wharf on the canal where rubbish is shot into waiting barges and the suicides hover in *Jipping Street* has a clear model in St Saviour's Wharf, on the Thames itself; but it is a fair walk from the street described here. Jipping Street was not real, and it is likely that its creator wanted us to recognise it as a state of mind, a slough of despond. Writing thirty years before Kathleen Woodward did, Arthur Morrison described the emotional topography of any poor London Street:

> . . . where in the East End lies this street? Everywhere. The hundred and fifty yards is only a link in a long and mightily tangled chain — is only a turn in the tortuous maze. The

street . . . is hundreds of miles long . . . there is no other way in the world that can more properly be called a single street, because of its dismal lack of accent, its sordid uniformity, its utter remoteness from delight . . .[7]

At the age of twelve, Kathleen Woodward found factory work on the north side of the river, and then, perhaps a couple of years later, returned to Bermondsey to work as a machinist in a clothing factory. This must have been about 1910 (*Jipping Street* is as vague about time as it is precise in its misleading topography), and the first external corroboration of her account concerns the years in the collar factory just before the war, described here in 'Escape'. When Kathleen Woodward published her first book, *Queen Mary*[8] in 1927, several newspapers took up her story at precisely the place where *Jipping Street* ends, recounting how 'a worker in a south London collar factory was rescued by the late Mary Macarthur, the trade union organiser and friend of the Queen'.[9]

Mary Macarthur, Secretary of the National Federation of Women Workers, was active in Bermondsey twice during the period when Kathleen Woodward was an adolescent worker there, first during the Bermondsey Uprising of 1911, when, inspired by the all-London walk-out by dockers, 'without any organisation, without any lead, thousands of (Bermondsey) workers, men, women and girls, came out on strike';[10] and again in 1913, when she worked to extend the provision of the National Insurance Act (1912) to the shirtmaking, food preserving and sugar confectionery industries – all Bermondsey trades that employed large numbers of women and girls.[11] It is likely that Mary Macarthur and Kathleen Woodward met during 1911 (the character of

ix

Miss Doremus in *Jipping Street* may well be a portrait of Mary Macarthur); but the precise nature of the 'rescue' performed by her is not yet clear. At the outbreak of war, Mary Macarthur was co-opted onto the Central Committee on Women's Employment, which was presided over by Queen Mary – sewing and knitting by ladies for the war effort was undercutting wages of women in the clothing industry. Mary Macarthur acted as the Committee's Honorary Secretary and there developed between her and the Queen what Kathleen Woodward in *Queen Mary* refers to as 'an extraordinarily romantic if unknown story called by certain women in the Labour Party "the case of Mary Ann and Mary R" (Regina).'

Mary Macarthur died in 1921, but, whatever the quality of her friendship with the author of *Jipping Street,* it is certain that the range of acquaintances she developed during the war years helped Kathleen Woodward obtain the interviews that made her first book such a success.

The closing date of *Jipping Street* is probably 1915, and the war provided its author with the means to get up and out. By 1925 she was living in a flat in Middle Temple, sharing with a female friend, an American law student. In the years after leaving Bermondsey she worked her passage across the Atlantic as a stewardess, worked as a receptionist at a London club, wrote children's stories, worked as a freelance journalist, and on the staff of the *Daily Express*.[12] She also spent some time after 1928 on the *New York Times*.

Kathleen Woodward converted to Catholicism in the 1930s and went on writing until her death in 1961. Her last book, *The Lady of Marlborough House* (a more elaborate version of *Queen Mary*) appeared in 1938.

When *Jipping Street*, her second book, appeared in 1928, reviewers used it to outline the early chapters of a romantic life. The publication of *Queen Mary* the year before had shown its author to be one who had already made the traditional journey of the fairy-tale, across the river, to the other side. She was 'the daughter of a washer-woman who grew up to be the biographer of a queen', 'a London factory hand who wrote the Queen's life.'[13] Amidst the rave reviews, both here and abroad,[14] some critics noted *Jipping Street's* oddness as auto-biography, and placed it on the literary borderlands of the novel. They were then able to read it in the tradition of the novel of 'low-life', or the semi-sociological reve-lations of books like Arthur Morrison's *Child of the Jago*,[15] and to see its pages peopled by lovable or horri-fying Dickensian characters.

Yet at each point of such characterisation, Kathleen Woodward takes her readers to the point of ironic conceit: the gentle Marxist basket maker – who slits a child's throat on Clapham Common; fast Lil, who gets her deserts and whose dead child is laid out in a *cake* box. It is as if the author taunts us with the possibility that it really could have been as bad as that, as if the goose girl in the fairy-tale were to casually pen in the chilling details of her life after the transformation had taken place, and she had already come to inhabit the royal palace. In fact, it becomes clear that, consciously or not, Kathleen Woodward wanted her readers to understand the tricks she played with autobiography and narrative, her reversals of topography, and her ironies of characterisation and literary allusion.

It was words that paid for Kathleen Woodward's

transformation across the river, and *Jipping Street* is a book about words, particularly words as escape routes. Like many of the men who later remembered their education through the socialist and free-thought groups of Edwardian London, she took to journalism. But she never came, as some of those men did, to condemn the lure of 'the beautiful words', nor to reject the blandishments of the eighteenth- and nineteenth-century classics by which they educated themselves, and the seductive elegancies of their prose. Teenagers of the 1900s, drunk on their own oratory, the rolling glory of their quotations, eschewed the sense and satisfied their souls with the sounds, seized wooden boxes and stood on them in the snow outside public houses, and uttered the beautiful, moving, sensuous words.[16] Kathleen Woodward's story is one of seduction and betrayal by the beautiful words. The sonorous repetitions of *Jipping Street* give the violent events she describes the ambiguous qualities of a dream, and the reader asks, against her will, was a grandmother *really* swung round the room by her hair? Did her mother *really* split the mad grandfather's back open with an axe?

Yet there is no ambiguity about the major relationships of this book. Kathleen Woodward's mother is the central character of *Jipping Street,* and the enabling and gentle figures of Jessica Mourn and Marian Evelyn throw into relief her daughter's stark portraiture. There is no mistaking what is meant in this account: Kathleen Woodward will allow no one to fall back on the myth of working-class motherhood.

Recent reinterpretations of psychoanalytic theory have provided striking accounts of the way in which the mothering of daughters produces in little girls the need and desire to mother in their turn. Accounts like that of Nancy Chodorow in *Mothering*[17] may come to be modified and extended by the case-history that is *Jipping Street,* for what results from the relationship between mother and daughter described here seems not to have been the need to mother, but the impossibility of Kathleen Woodward's reproducing herself. On the evidence of *Jipping Street* she knew as a child that she was a burden to her mother, that she need never have been born, that mothers could indeed kill their children. The child shrank from sexual knowledge, from an understanding of a process that had brought her into being, and that gave women 'so little pleasure, so little joy'.

The contradiction of knowing as a child that whilst one exists, one also need never have been, is a great impetus to thought, a fine honing for a child's intelligence; but it implies as well, a death of sensuality. What has been indicated in books like *Maternity: Letters from Working Women*[18] is here made a little plainer. We need to know more, perhaps by a different reading of the few texts of working-class womanhood that we already possess, of what the implications for sexuality are of this particular psychological history.

*Jipping Street* indicates what this psychological history might be, and its value as evidence may well lie in the places where it breaks the rules of autobiography. In autobiographical narration, what matters is the order and veracity of the events described. To reverse the order is to falsify the account; to omit something is to alter it.[19] The autobiographical narrator presents herself as a witness to real events. It is therefore possible to tell lies in autobiography, to bear false historical witness, in a way that it is not possible to tell lies in the writing of a novel. However, in the construction of a psychological narrative – in the making of case-history – truth and order do not matter in the same way. If the events described are falsified, the reader still ends up with the same story in the end: the individual's account of how she got to be the way she is.[20] The events described carry their own meaning. A happening or a relationship may be removed from its 'real' context, and described in another setting; but any falsification this may involve does not alter the status of events and relationships as psychological evidence, though questions must certainly be raised about them as historical truth. Ideas and feelings have, after all, to be embodied in some way; the particularity of *Jipping Street* is that its author uses working-class life and socialist politics to embody hers, rather than the cultural referents that we are accustomed to from traditional case-history.

If *Jipping Street* is to be read in this way, then it deserves the status of underground literature, for it tells a story that neither the confines of descriptive sociology nor the new structures of feminism can allow. It is about the ambivalence and restriction of the relationship between mother and daughter, about a mother no longer split in to good and bad as in the fairy-tales and psychoanalytic theory, but powerfully integrated, terribly confining. It is a corrective, written fifty years ago, to all those recent accounts that seek to define the mother/daughter relationship as one of nourishment and support; and it is a salutary reminder that class circumstances alter psychological cases.

Ellen Woodward displayed the stoicism and endurance that has been described as the rationalisation of oppression.[21] Often, her façade of endurance cracked, and she expressed herself in extreme violence towards her children. The child Kathleen accepted the physical violence calmly, but she violently rejected the dreary stoicism of her mother's vision: 'shut your mouth and go on.' This is a book about being the daughter of such a mother. It is about all those mothers who tell you, impossibly, that it is unbearable, but that it has to be borne . . . 'If only there were not Jipping Street, and the factory, and mother . . .'; intolerable burden, impossible legacy.

*Carolyn Steedman, Leamington Spa, 1982*

## Notes

1. Jean McCrindle and Sheila Rowbotham, *Dutiful Daughters,* Penguin, Harmondsworth, 1979, p. 116; p. 4.
2. Joy Parr, *Labouring Children,* Croom Helm, London, 1980, pp. 14–26; James Walvin, *A Child's World,* Penguin, Harmondsworth, 1982, pp. 61–69; Carol Dyhouse, *Girls Growing up in Late Victorian and Edwardian England,* Routledge and Kegan Paul, London, 1981, pp. 104–105.
3. T.A. Jackson, *Solo Trumpet,* Lawrence & Wishart, London, 1953; Guy A. Aldred, *No Traitors' Gait* (3 vols.), Strickland Press, Glasgow, 1955–1963; R.M. Fox, *Smoky Crusade,* Hogarth Press, London, 1937; Edward Royle, *Radicals, Secularists & Republicans: Popular Freethought in Britain 1866–1915,* MUP, Manchester, 1982.
4. Gareth Stedman-Jones, 'Working Class Culture & Working Class Politics in London, 1870–1900', *Journal of Social History,* 7 (1974) pp. 460–508.
5. Rupert E. Davies, *John Scott Lidgett,* Epworth Press, London, 1957, p. 54.
6. Alexander Paterson, *Across the Bridges,* Edward Arnold, London, 1911.
7. Arthur Morrison, *Tales of Mean Streets* (1894), Methuen & Co., London, 1903, Introduction.

8. Kathleen Woodward, *Queen Mary: A Life & Intimate Study,* Hutchinson, London, 1927.

9. *Daily Mail,* 20.9.27.

10. Fenner Brockway, *Bermondsey Story: The Life of Alfred Salter,* Allen & Unwin, London, 1949, pp. 46–48.

11. Mary Agnes Hamilton, *Mary Macarthur: A Biographical Sketch,* Leonard Parsons, London, 1925, pp. 101–107; pp. 120–121.

12. *Daily Mail, Daily Express, Daily Sketch,* 20.9.27; *World's Children* November 1928. Records of the National Union of Journalists.

13. Copy for Longman's edition, 1928; *The Adelaide Register,* November 17, 1928.

14. *Jipping Street* was simultaneously published in the USA by Harper Row.

15. Arthur Morrison, *Child of the Jago* (1896), Methuen, London, 1897.

16. Jackson, Aldred, Fox, *op. cit.*

17. Nancy Chodorow, *Mothering, Psychoanalysis and the Reproduction of Gender,* University of California Press, Berkeley, 1978.

18. Margaret Llewelyn Davies, *Maternity: Letters from Working Women* (1915), Virago Press, London, 1978.

19. William Labov, *Language in the Inner City,* University of Pennsylvania Press, Philadelphia, 1974, pp. 364–393.

20. Jonathan Culler, *The Pursuit of Signs,* Routledge and Kegan Paul, London, 1981, pp. 128–181.

21. Sigmund Freud, The Pelican Freud Library (9) *Case Histories II,* Penguin, 1979, pp. 287–290.

22. Anna Pollert, *Girls, Wives, Factory Lives,* Macmillan, London, 1980, pp. 121–122.

Professor Hamish Miles of the Barber Institute of Fine Arts, Birmingham University and Mrs Elizabeth Grey both talked to me about their memories of Kathleen Woodward. I am extremely grateful for their help. My thanks as well to Raphael Samuel, Anna Davin and Bill Livingstone for reading *Jipping Street* and providing me with background information.

# I

# THE "WORLD ON ITS TOES"

# I

THE circumstances of my mother's life in no manner differ from the circumstances of the lives of those inarticulate people without number who compose the " lower " classes. She was born in poverty; she was acquainted all her days with the insecurity and uncertainty which are the heritage of the poor. She knew, she said, only two certain things: death—and the landlord; and for her the dawn of each new day was cast over by the pale shifting face of want.

Her life was as bare of exceptional events as her inheritance was innocent of distinction: she could read only the simplest words, and wrote her name with much difficulty. Nature had shaped her, Nature as she breeds in the byways and alleys of great cities: crude, dumb, brutal, kind, unlovely, unalloyed. A common lot she had, and lived a common life, and she remains for me one of the most singular and individual women I have ever known.

Singular, for example, in her strength and poise, for my mother had that strength and poise which comes to those without hope and without fear.

I think she must once have known hope, when she was young and had large grey eyes, even white teeth, hair black as jet, a full, laughing mouth, and a straight, live, eager body, whose eagerness you could clearly see in the old photograph we had, where she was eighteen and wore a frock full of the oddest flounces and tucks which strove to conceal the live, warm, eager lines.

I think then she must have known hope.

She was born and grew up in a back room behind Cloth Fair, within the sound of Bow Bells and the smell of the meat in Smithfield Markets; and she loved her mother with a passionate love made fierce and protective by the unbelievable cruelties inflicted on them both by her father.

A later generation would have called my grandfather mad; my mother and my grandmother thought him simply bad, and after he had bruised and trampled on their lives, he drowned himself in the Thames, to the inexpressible relief of them both.

4

His body was recovered at Mortlake; and mother always spoke with pride of the fact that my grandmother, having sworn that she would never look on his face again, refused even to identify his body in the mortuary. I never heard one good thing about him.

By a strange irony, one of the few pictures that lightened our walls in Jipping Street was a framed certificate of his death, on which also was recorded the fact that his body was washed up at Mortlake. This solitary memorial held for me a most fearful interest.

I like to think that mother once knew hope— when she had even white teeth and a laughing mouth and live, warm, eager lines, though she soon put away hope and fear and grew to suffer life as it came each day with a fine, flinty endurance; hardened in suffering, without illusions as she was without hope; enduring in proud obstinacy, without fear. Proud, obstinate, fearless, without hope and without that last noble extremity of courage which dares to hope.

" Life kicks you downstairs and then it kicks you upstairs," she said; for so it had been with her, numbing the warm, eager lines, now

5

passionless, stony, and distorted beyond all loveliness and form.

The cruel, ugly unrefinement of suffering!

" Pulled this way and that with that dead child I was; pulled inside out; everybody in the room bobbing up and down: ' For the sake of God Almighty let me die!' They said I tore the doctor's coat in shreds. Fifteen weeks I was in bed after that dead child; had to crawl down the stairs on my back when I got better. . . ."

Oh the cruel unrefinement of suffering!

I used to think of the dead child in bed at night, before I went to sleep, and it would fill me with horror and suffocating fear; and in the darkness I could see mother sliding down the stairs on her back, white, trembling, to cut up bread for the children's tea; and, stronger than the fear and the suffocating horror, there would well up in me a deep, surging passion of growth toward her.

Full of tears, and resolution, I would at last fall asleep on the damp pillow.

Fearless and without hope mother was; flinty, enduring, strong, proud; she did not ask and she did not receive; the suffering had bitten in until it was itself impotent against the granite it laid bare.

Dimly from my earliest childhood I was aware of this, and it made me catch my breath in a confusion of awe and wonder.

Six children she reluctantly bore, and she was in the habit of saying in a curiously passionless tone that if she had known as much when her first child was born as she learned by the time she bore her sixth, a second child would never have been.

Greatly in sympathy with mother, and in no little perplexity, I cried often with Job: "Why, then, was I ever born?"

"God only knows," mother would say, and rest the problem there, while I found neither knowledge nor consolation in her answer, for to me it was clear that if we children had never been born mother's life would have been as an absurd dream of continued ease.

Not that she whined about us, or complained; she spoke truly as she felt, regretting each one of us come to a world filled with anxiety and numberless hours of toil. She never lied about her feeling; she made no pretences; she said that all we had to do was to shut our mouths and go on.

7

I could not discover in my own self either her grim acceptance of life or her rigid endurance, and my days were spent in a bewilderment on unresolved protests, questionings and problems. I could and I did conceive of a world that was wholly different; and this was a torment no less than a relief.

Listening to mother, life seemed a long-drawn-out agony of uncertainty, rounded off by death and possibly the workhouse, which was worse than death. The terror for me, however, lay beyond rather than in the immediate present, where mother was, for I could not imagine a happening that would break down her obstinate endurance.

She was eighteen when she met my father and married him, and gave the reasons for her marriage with a rare and admirable veracity. She married him, she said, for a little quiet; for a rest and change from the turbulent life of the back room behind Cloth Fair, where my grandfather, affecting an extreme puritanism in his morals, beat them, and broke up the few sticks which composed their home, and once swung my grandmother round the room by her hair. It was on this occasion that my mother split

open his back with a chopper. I have no doubt
that he deserved the blow, and I never thought
to question whatever my mother did; but I
discovered in myself a shrinking from the chopper story, and a degree of wonder at mother's
steady, consistent satisfaction in this particular
event.

The chopper came to symbolise for me the
hardships and cruelties of all her early days and
the days of my grandmother.

My father was tall and slender, and summed
up in his person the qualities my grandfather was
notably without: he was exquisitely gentle and
sensitive; he was refined without being cultured;
quiet, retiring, having in him a certain quality
which drew to him men, women and children.
He retained his sensibilities and his charm
through all his adversities: in squalor, poverty,
want and ugliness unredeemed, his coat was
brushed to a thread, his boots patched and
polished. He bathed regularly, and with infinite
difficulty, in a small hand-basin; he refrained
from the common vulgarity of speech which
surrounded him, and was consistently fastidious
in his habits.

I remember that he refused to eat from a

bare, untidy table; and I can see him carefully brushing away the litter, and since we had no tablecloth, he would supply this want with a newspaper, delicately spread out on the table.

He had in addition to his natural fastidiousness an air, a manner of wearing his clothes which gave distinction to the shabbiest black suit, musty coloured with age, threadbare; and in his presence the neighbours in Jipping Street instinctively checked their oaths and vulgarities. They respected his intrinsic refinement and delicacy, and sympathised with his obvious physical suffering, and when they spoke of him among themselves they called him a "gentleman."

My mother had hardly been married when he fell sick with an illness which left him half invalid for the rest of his life; and my mother's bright prospects for rest and a change were thus rudely and abruptly set aside.

From that time on my mother became the stay and support of the home, and my father endured, in addition to untold bodily suffering, the peculiar torment of looking on helpless while my mother shouldered her superhuman burdens.

This made his life an exquisite torment, for, if he was gentle, he had a proud, independent spirit, and he united to the sensibilities of a woman a virile and manly conception of his duties and responsibilities.

Increasing anxieties, the sense of his own impotence and infirmities, slowly crushed the life out of him.

He was born and brought up in circumstances unlike the circumstances of my mother's birth and early life; he scarcely knew of the existence of those hardships with which she was very familiar. He had known the comfort and security of a home; he had been sheltered by a tender and solicitous mother; his upbringing was gentle.

I know little else; for the subject of his early life did not move my mother to conversation, and my father never referred to it.

You must see mother as she most familiarly comes back to me: From out of the wash-house in Jipping Street, for ever full of damp, choking, soapy steam from the copper, which settles on the broken window panes and in a moment becomes a thousand little rivulets falling drunkenly down the surface of the windows, and hangs in tiny, tremulous drops on the ledges which I can watch as I wait to turn the wringer. I wait, and watch the steam on the window, and listen to mother.

Out of the steam comes mother's face—pinkish purple, sweating, her black hair putting forth lank wisps that hang over her forehead and cling to the nape of her neck. The hairpins in her hair rust in the damp and steam.

" Christ! " she gasps, and wipes the sweat from her face, and for a few moments rests her hands on the side of the wash-tub—hands unnaturally crinkled and bleached from the stinging soda water.

" Wash, wash, wash; it's like washing your guts away. Stand, stand, stand; I want six pairs of feet; and then I'd have to stand on my head to give them a rest. . . ."

I eagerly looked forward to those nights when we left the wash-house at nine to take home the finished washing and collect more washing.

Down Jipping Street we went, round the hospital bend, over the interminable London Bridge carrying the bundle of washing in turn—the clean-smelling, soapy clean washing—the insufferable day behind us.

When we got to Mrs. Moody's in Thames
Street we wedged our feet in the front door lest
it be shut in our faces without the washing
money, and our emotions were divided between
the agonising uncertainty of Mrs. Moody's
finances and the inexpressible relief of the day
behind us.

On our way home we stopped at the " World
On Its Toes," where mother had a glass of beer,
and life took on a different look in the warm
smell of fresh beer and sawdust; the gaslights
turned full on, and everybody being friendly, at
ease, and telling secrets to each other, and confidences. Nellie the barmaid would be pinked
up and shrill, her unmanageable bosom pro-
tuding grossly over the bar counter; and we
could sit on the form in the public bar for as
long as mother could possibly take to drink her
glass of beer; and from where I sat I could look
at the sponge cakes under a glass vase on the
bar shelf, cakes that you could eat until you
again felt hungry—only, no one could afford so
many sponge cakes.

After the long day, with the background of
the " World On Its Toes," mother's face often
comes back to me, and she sighs with a sort of

13

contentment, and sips her beer, and there are six or seven hours between her and the scrubbing brush to-morrow.

A sip of beer at a time. Quietly she licks her lips; but there would remain a brown rim over her upper lip which, when the sipping was over, she would wipe away as a last gesture. Finis.

Rare relaxation in the " World On Its Toes!" Nellie the barmaid bulging, abandoned; a challenge and an invitation, and very kind to children; rings on her fingers. " Pity she can't get rings on her thumbs," mother said dryly. Queer canker marks the rings left on her fingers. A bulging vision of high colour and Plenty; and they said that Nellie put soot on her eyebrows to accentuate them, and docked the half-pint glasses to pay for dye for her hair, and received as many confidences as she received free drinks; and was like a pawnshop in that she " took in anything." A bursting, Olympian vision, with tiny feet, encased in patent-leather boots buttoned at the side, and a loud, frequent laugh. Mother tired from the day and sobered by the knowledge of to-morrow relaxing in the warm smell of fresh beer and sawdust and the gaslights turned full on. These things create her mood—detached, sombre. Such nights, over her glass of beer in the "World On Its Toes," she would relent and talk of the Past: about the dead child, and father—pale-face, gentle father, mysteriously withdrawn in sickness; father with the sunken eyes filled with tears because he is too ill to go out and work. Mother is saying he should have been a woman, for he is so delicate and ill and sensitive and anxious.

I try to think of him, and faintly, in the heavy swooning odour of the lavender flowers mother used to burn in his sick-room, I can hear the sound of his voice, low, broken, quivering, coming through the bedroom door:

"What have I done to deserve this? What have I done?"

Dear God, what has father done? I am sitting on the stairs outside the bedroom door supplicating, questioning, upbraiding God—waiting for mother, too afraid to go to bed. I know that he is holding on tightly to her as though to save himself from slipping into the arms of Death; and it is easy to understand that Death itself might be intimidated by mother, who looks unswervingly ahead, with a shut mouth and hard lines in her face; and divides her days

between holding father back from the grave—
and the wash-tub—and the scrubbing-brush—
and occasional excursions, as when we went on
that bleak November morning before the Board
of Guardians.

Only once did I, personally, appear before the
Guardians of the Parish. Mother went out to
scrub from six o'clock in the morning till noon.
We "took in" washing from noon until night, but
there being five of us to feed, and we being always
hungry, the slightest falling-off of the supply of
washing threatened our slender resources. On
occasions when the washing was slack the local
Guardians, in our extremity, gave us relief.

The relief they gave us was rice, a weekly
sum of rice. We ate rice until we were sick from
eating rice, when my mother modestly appealed
for a little change, and in consequence we were
summoned peremptorily before the Board of
Guardians, mother and we five.

I did not like the twelve men and women
seated about the table, and hung tightly to
mother who, as usual, seemed a pillar of strength
and was, no doubt, sick with apprehension. I
recall how the bleak, uncompromising light of
that November morning dealt mercilessly with

the faces of the twelve men and women Guardians; how mother's face whitened and hardened as the Board fired question after question and she grew more dogged, and less able to show cause why we should not continue eating rice. Presently, a very sunburnt lady, who to mother's untutored eye looked positively mulatto, said, with insolence and finality:

" Rice is very nutritious! "

" It may be where you come from," mother retorted with desperate incisiveness, whereupon we were incontinently hurried from the presence of the Board, and returned home to an unvarying diet of rice.

Life might have been less difficult for my mother if she had been able to relax her pride, if she had been more hesitating, more diffident in the presence of her " superiors "—like the Guardians, and the local clergyman who was the distributing centre of " food tickets " supplied to the poor by benevolent persons outside Bermondsey. Superior persons of this kind, however, provoked her to the utmost contempt and impatience, and ground a fine edge to her tongue. To expedience she was, I think, a complete stranger.

17

Our local clergyman was a pious person with a finicky, girlish manner, and a most exaggerated concern for the welfare of the soul. He had—this fount of food tickets and spiritual succour—an attenuated person and a sickly look, which caused my mother to christen him " The Churchyard Deserter."

He was much cultivated in Jipping Street for the food tickets he had to bestow; and my mother was the only person I knew who did not think it a good bargain to exchange her condition of sin for some tea, sugar and bread, with sometimes a little meat thrown in to weight the scales.

I lived close to my mother, held fast by strong ties which existed without love or affection; indissolubly I was bound.

And I shall never know how much strength and resolution she gave to me. She gave me courage; and from her I learned to hide my fear, however little I might learn not to be afraid.

I humbly acknowledge my debt to her, although I can never know really its nature or dimension.

She nursed only one softness in her heart, a tenderness for my father. Him she sustained in body and in soul, without being conscious of the sacrifices she made, the giving out; she gave without question.

She sweated and laboured for her children, equally without stint or thought, but was utterly oblivious to any need we might cherish for sympathy in our little sorrows, support in our strivings. She simply was not aware of anything beyond the needs of our bodies.

In her anger, which was frequent and violent —for when she touched that extreme verge of tiredness in mind and body and would not give way it seemed to revenge itself and become a fierce anger—she aimed her blows without feeling or restraint. Once she split my head open; and again she threw a fork at me, which dangerously pierced my side.

Violent she could be, ungovernable in her rage, but she never was mean. I have nursed many a scar and wound she inflicted on my body, and, for a week on end, have nursed bruises for some childish misdemeanour, but I have never felt a moment of animosity toward her, or been conscious of the suspicion of a feeling of bitterness.

Her chastisement was, as it were, clean and honest, and in keeping with her nature.

She had no love to give us and, thank God, she never pretended what she did not feel; but children miss the presence of love and wilt, when they are not embittered, in its absence.

At home it was always wintry.

# II

# JESSICA MOURN

I COME inevitably to Jipping Street where I was born and where I grew up, my background and my foreground; and it seemed to me until I left Jipping Street, when I was about thirteen, to take up the sobering responsibilities of earning a living on the far side of London Bridge, that all the world was a continuation, an expansion of Jipping Street. It bounded my horizon, and I tremble when I consider Jipping Street in the light of our ever-advancing psychology; for the psychologist would give us as little reason to hope as the theologian he would displace, if it be true that early influences are so potent, so impressing, so inescapable. I hardly know if there is much to choose between being born in sin— or Jipping Street.

Threading the heart of Bermondsey, it winds from London Bridge to the Old Kent Road, and although it is acknowledged as a short cut to many points of activity—to London Bridge and

Tooley Street, to St. George's Church and the Borough—people avoid it for the longer way by the canal bank, which runs parallel with the street.

We were never wantonly invaded, save by the smell of the hops brewing at the foot of London Bridge, from which you might have thought that industry was confined to the manufacture of beer; but this was not so: there were three tanyards about the neighbourhood, and a pickle factory off Ben Rents; there was, too, a jam factory which at times seasoned the air with the odour of fruits fermenting, and we knew the hour from piercing shrieks released from the funnel of the jam factory three times a day.

On the far side of the canal there was a wharf where paper was made from old rags; the Vestry stood close to the wharf, and here refuse was legitimately collected, and shot into the waiting barges.

You might, at times, catch the smell of the hospital reared on an ancient site at the far end of Jipping Street, a few steps from London Bridge, the insistent, nauseating smell of chloroform.

The abiding smell of Jipping Street, however,

the pitch and tone, was set by the breweries at the foot of London Bridge; and it was only after you had been long in the neighbourhood that you became aware, at intervals, of the smell of fruits fermenting, the odorous processes of tan, intermingled with the faint insidious waves of chloroform.

Two and three-roomed houses were reared unbrokenly up each side of Jipping Street; the street was long and narrow, and the substance of a house dissolved on the slightest provocation; frequently the half or whole of someone's ceiling fell in, and regularly every Monday the landlord's agent came to collect the rents. This was not an easy labour for the landlord's agent.

We took pride in the hospital on the ancient site at the far end of Jipping Street, we clung to this one fearful difference between us and the other streets in Bermondsey, long and winding, poverty-struck.

There, by the hospital, Horror walked briskly up and down stark, without cloth or covering, and Pain writhed and anguished past on a police ambulance, crowds swarming after— men, women, children, irresistibly drawn; and Suffering—mysterious, consuming, physical

Suffering—displayed no lineament new or strange to our eyes.

Shading the courtyard of the hospital on the ancient site were three great plane trees, breathing the promise of God in their fresh, moist leaves. Sometimes, broad-smiling, the sunlight lay aslant through the leaves, or danced like lovely dream children on the courtyard; and between the plane trees and the worn, mellow walls of the hospital there seemed to live a perfect understanding.

At night the starlings held concert in the trees, twittering shrilly away through the quiet dreadful spaces of the night—restless, loquacious, as if to break that stilly silence which broods heavily about the presence of suffering and pain. All night the starlings twittered shrilly to heighten the ghostly quiet.

In Jipping Street we were never wantonly invaded save by the smell of the hops brewing, the swooning odour of chloroform from the hospital, and the smell of the tanyards; the police ambulance hurrying swiftly past, crowds after the ambulance, and, through the day and through the night, a broken procession of visitors to the hospital: " cases," and those visiting " cases."

So plainly you could hear the hurrying feet through the night, pattering down Jipping Street, communicating the anxious, throbbing beat of the heart; in the day, drawn faces, unaware of Jipping Street, and spurred on by some nameless apprehension, continually passed. You could see them come home, with a grief that was known, but withholding its sharpest pain until the first lethe touch had spent its numb self: they walked through Jipping Street as in a dream.

When I was a child I believed, for it was repeatedly said, that the hospital existed to " do things with knives "; and I remember the talk occasioned by the melancholy fate of Maggie Murphy, who lived next door to us, and went into the hospital for an operation on her ears, and came out without her tonsils, having somehow got mixed up with the tonsil cases.

Maggie went in a second time to be cut about the ears.

We had two rooms in a three-roomed house at the hospital end of Jipping Street. Our back window commanded a view of the canal, that peremptory escape for the more impatient spirits in the neighbourhood, of whom there were not a few. Sometimes people came from far off to drown themselves in the canal, and a week seemed not to pass without yielding up the body of one suicide; and the Police, or the Coroner, or some mysterious officer awarded you twelve shillings and sixpence for each body recovered, and nothing at all for rescuing a live person; which seemed ironical on the part of the Police, or the Coroner, or the power concerned in these awards.

At night in the dark the canal took on a gaunt sighing beauty, the cranes on the wharf-side starkly silhouetted, the black outlines of the barges dimly to be seen in the black water, for ever lapping against their immovable sides.

Remote, still, untroubled it lay, receiving with calm the tired spirit creeping from some corner to the embosoming waters.

I used to sit by the window and resolve strange moving shapes and forms in the dissolving lines of the barges and cranes on the wharf-side.

It was less lovely in the garish light of day, with the refuse from the Borough so indifferently shot into the waiting barges that it defiled the face of the canal for days on end. The clatter and groan of the cranes rasped unceasingly in the

air, and there was never a moment's pause except
when a body was being rescued from the be-
fouled waters.

The body was laid on the bank and rudely
covered with an old coat, or tarpaulin, while
awaiting the Police ambulance to take it to the
mortuary; and the crowd would grow with every
passing moment, and each newcomer peeped
at the waxen face, and variously apostrophised
God in His heaven, and the Mother of Jesus,
and the talk would grow louder, and the specu-
lation more curious—heedless of the still, in-
curious face under the covering.

Soon the clatter and groans of the cranes
would again fill the air with their rasping notes
and, having had our fill of death, we came back
to the business of life.

I spent most of my childhood in the street,
for we could not assemble in the two rooms with
comfort.

When I think of Jipping Street I think of
Jessica Mourn; gently, insistently her image
takes shape in the mists of the past, and she is
sitting in her front parlour looking on Jipping
Street, hands folded lightly in her lap, her face
wearing its constant expression of sad repose—

a pale, tranquil face, set with two brown eyes that commonly express a " something," Poppy Lapum said, that she had once seen in the eyes of a dog run over in Jipping Street: an observation fixed in my mind.

There was, however, more than mute appeal in the eyes of Jessica Mourn; they seemed to mirror all the sufferings of Bermondsey they had looked on; serene in their sadness, grave, composed, you looked on them, received their benediction and felt strangely absolved, at rest.

I see her skimpy brown hair tightly knotted at the back and kept in place with one pin, a feat of which she was proud; and the weight of her hair, as she remarked from time to time, did not make her head ache. Her feet are contained in the neatest spring-side boots; and she wears her white apron, so stiffly starched that it can neither crease nor fold nor otherwise shape itself to her person, but must needs advance and retreat like strong cardboard. There is then her black shawl, a part of her inalienable as the white apron, and which by some elusive quality lends itself to thought and feeling as she now retires into its depths and again emerges and ceaselessly twitches it about the shoulders. . . .

Now it is summer and I see her standing at her front door, a part of Jipping Street yet strangely detached, and as the evening lengthens there is a poetry in her brooding presence; she stands motionless, wrapped in her black shawl, and an aura of deep quiet that rebukes the shrill unresting street. On her brow sublimity sits, the reward of sufferings that have armoured her against hope and left her the more vulnerable to the sufferings of others. Now and then she sighs, gently meditating, no doubt, on some new grief that has come to her parlour; for Jipping Street brings to her its woes and tribulations: her horizon is bounded by sadness and affliction.

When I was a child I used to sit in Jessica's front parlour whenever it was possible; she was my refuge and my shelter; and she had about her an inexpressible tenderness and that refinement which grows out of a soul laid away in suffering.

Her tenderness stands out in relief against the bleak Spartan tone of my own home and my mother's impatience with the outward forms of affection. She had suffered and grown hard; it was not so with Jessica Mourn. Her tenderness and her compassion were divinely inexhaustible;

and they were the abiding wonder of all my childhood.

Jessica had a distaste for the Present; her refuge was in the Past. She spoke of the future as an unfortunate, howbeit certain, continuing of the Present, sinking impalpably into a deep sleep, for which she would be glad; this bred in her a philosophy of patience and enduring.

From confidences rarely given, and cherished in their meaning for Jessica, I became acquainted with her Past; with the facts, the events of that Past which, uninformed by her faith and ardour, unaccompanied by those upward glances of the eye as though she were at her devotions, without the long pregnant pauses and the changing face of the shawl, seem barren indeed, and forlorn.

Jessica's mother made brushes in one of the basements in Kent Street, and here Jessica was born. There loitered through the gratings on the street pavement a little light, a little air, but you could not see the sky unless you came up from the basement when you were unsteadied by the revelation. The world walked overhead and rattled the gratings as it passed down the street.

Jessica did not know her father, for her mother was " married but not churched," as they said, meaningly, in Jipping Street. She was, however, informed on other circumstances of her birth, for it seems to have made a lasting impression on her mother's mind, and, as she looked to the corner of the basement, she would be moved to speak to Jessica of the event.

Late at night, and while overhead in Kent Street a battle was raging between the Gellham and Roper clans, Jessica came to the basement to the sound of shrieking women and cursing men and the steady rhythm of police truncheons laying the combatants before them.

Perhaps Jessica never altogether recovered from this first surprise; for she sickened, was querulous as a baby, and seemed ready, at the merest whim, to flit fretfully away.

In course of time she was put out on the pavement to take the air in common with the other babies in Kent Street, and here she developed, among a succession of childish complaints, a habit of preternatural quiet. Since it was the faith of Kent Street that a quiet baby was an unnatural baby, she was often shaken out of her settled calm.

33

Jessica's mother was much given to dreaming and the stuff of her dreams she got from penny novelettes bought at the rag shop where for a penny they gave a generous if old and tattered pile. These lent colour and glamour to the facts of life reflected in the basement—to the "shameful" fact of Jessica—and she came more and more to recline in the corner reading her novelettes in the pale light of the gratings, while Jessica twisted fibre for the brushes and never tired of the stories her mother re-created, stories of strange passions and unhappy loves.

Jessica often said, fondly, that her mother could "put more hooks and eyes" on a story than anyone she knew; and I recall how the unearthly but impassioned creatures of her imagining, stored in Jessica's memory, varied our evenings in Jipping Street.

Jessica could not read or write, but names, persons, places, with the stories her mother told her, were graven enduringly in her mind. She had wanted to learn to read, but there was no one to teach her except her mother, who seemed to fall short of the practical effort entailed; and Jessica was left to lament all her life that she could not read or write, and to

34

give a most exaggerated importance to these proficiencies.

Soon she came to do all the work in the basement and they were happy together cloistered under the earth and not unaware of affairs on the surface of Kent Street, which contrasted vividly with their own sedate lives: there was continued fighting overhead—and women who went forth at night, and lived in the Roper's dosshouses.

Roper's Go-Easy's! They seemed ever present in Jessica's talk of the Past to lend the lurid touch, and vein with horror the panorama of Kent Street which had scarcely lost its last lingering fragrances of the Canterbury Pilgrims who passed that way when Harriet Roper, Founder of the Roper line, chose it for the site of her first lodging-house.

Stories of this Harriet Roper were handed down from generation to generation in Kent Street. " We took 'em in with our milk," Jessica said. " Those of us that took milk. I always had a delicate stomach."

Harriet Roper bequeathed to her son three thriving dosshouses and a reputation for having had " as much brass in her face as would have

made a brass bedstead jealous." Many Ropers
were born, and died, leaving the fame of Harriet
the founder unimpaired; and one Roper was
hanged for murder. The passing of a Roper would
gather all Bermondsey in Kent Street, for Harriet had set a high standard in funerals, and it
was said that she ordered so many carriages to
follow her coffin to its burial-place a mile and
more from Kent Street that the first carriage
reached the cemetery before the last carriage
left Kent Street.

Jessica had seen the passing of 'Erb Roper,
last of the Roper line; and in a few masterly
touches, with many pregnant twitches of the
shawl, she would conjure up for me the crowds
collected in Kent Street; the cortège of black
funeral horses prancing tremulously up the
street as though the way were lined with iron
spikes; the sound of their bronchial whinny-
ings that brought up the goose-flesh on every
one present; the hushed " blimeys " of the men
and the gasps of the women as wreath after
wreath was piled on the coffin until at last you
could not see the coffin for flowers. Sighing, she
would conclude: " If you were asking me, I say
he'd want a Covent Garden to get him in right

with them what's above." And she would cast her eyes to the heavens and look sceptical.

Three generations of Ropers had passed away when Jessica was born in Kent Street, leaving their mark in the faces of the children and broken-down houses that took on a more evil look than the men and women who lived in them. From the south side of the river, by London Bridge, from the four corners of Bermondsey, came human refuse in the wake of Harriet Roper, and it settled about Kent Street, filling the doss-houses and bringing terror by day and night and continued trade for the Roper clan.

Their descendants filled the pockets of 'Erb Roper and continued the dreadful reputation of Kent Street, and as Jessica said, not without a touch of pride, " in them days no one policeman ever walked alone through Kent Street."

These were her mother's neighbours, living their incredible lives overhead, and dying violent deaths, while down in the basement Jessica made the brushes and her mother read novelettes, and between them was the world created in the imagination of Jessica's mother, a world no less incredible than that raging overhead and rattling the gratings as it passed down the street.

They came up from the basement for funerals, which were frequent and composed the one interest strongly binding Kent Street; they came up from the basement when a street fight seemed to promise the death of at least one or more; they had friendly words with the neighbours through the gratings, and they met at the water-butts and in the fried fish shop and when they were loading the barrow of finished brushes for Jessica to take to the City. These fleeting contacts with Kent Street and the neighbours were unreal to them and infrequent, and they retired hastily to the peace and security of the basement, Jessica to her brushes, her mother to the novelettes.

Jessica grew ill from time to time and this broke the even tenour of their days. Once she went to see Dr. Acton, who said that her blood had " got pale," that she must come up from the basement more often to take the air; and so it happened that in intervals of making brushes Jessica, for her health, scrubbed out empty houses. It was arduous work for one inured to the sedentary bench, but on the surface of the ground she got more air, and the doctor was kindly and sympathetic. Jessica never spoke of him without remarking: " He was our Saviour's footsteps over again."

So the years passed, thirty in all, when calamity in the shape of Mr. Mourn slouched into the Kent Street basement, rolling his shag fags and " spitting home-like " about the place, while Jessica little dreamed that romance was so near; Mr. Mourn seems to have borne little resemblance to the airy heroes who peopled the basement, called up by her mother's imaginings.

He was a stocky little man of the " bruiser " type not uncommon in Kent Street; and his mother lived in a basement higher up by the Borough, and had often talked to Jessica and her mother about her sailor son; for Mr. Mourn was a sailor, and Jessica was at first much unsteadied by the strong odour of the sea which seemed to cling about his person and in his sailor suit. She had not seen the sea save through the imagination of her mother, but this made it the more potent.

He came again to the basement and again and, although he was a man given to few words, told them stories of the sea, and his seafarings abroad, helped out by Jessica's mother, who lent the wild touch, the language of romance; while

Jessica seems to have pursued her gentle way with that detachment of manner habitual to her, and which she quickly recovered after Mr. Mourn's third or fourth visit. This did not at all please her mother, who was frankly disturbed by Jessica's gentle indifference to any and every young man who whistled down the gratings, or came to see them in the basement, as did Mr. Mourn.

She resolved that Jessica should be "churched" and " housed," and, to this end, promoted a correspondence between her daughter and Mr. Mourn when the time came for him to resume his navigations abroad.

Jessica's love letters were written by her mother, and I do not know if it was in consequence of these letters or not, but Mr. Mourn severed his connections with the sea, and came home to " settle down "; and soon, to Jessica's utmost surprise, she was " churched " to Mr. Mourn; and together they went to the front parlour in Jipping Street.

Her mother remained in the basement, framed and hung Jessica's marriage " lines " on the wall for Kent Street to see through the gratings, if it chose, and then one night she abruptly passed away in peace, the fullness of years, and with an unfailing sight.

They found a candle by her bedside, and a novelette, and an expression of fulfilment on her face which comforted Jessica in her grief. Jessica was left alone with the reality of Mr. Mourn in the parlour in Jipping Street.

From their first month together in the Jipping Street parlour, Mr. Mourn seems to have been irked by Jessica's gentle retiringness and quiet habit, while Jessica, never much given to words, was shocked into an almost unbroken silence by the revelation of Mr. Mourn.

Once he knocked her down for sitting still and saying nothing, and at the hospital on the ancient site they put stitches in her head.

His anger increased and spread to all the neighbours in Jipping Street, for, at one time or another, he engaged each one in battle.

" Mother could have told him stories," Jessica would reflect to me, sadly; " I was only a punch-ball, but it kept him in practice."

She withdrew more and more into her self, and she thought of her mother, and the halcyon days of Kent Street, and the basement; and now her life seemed suspended in a horror she could

not understand and felt she could not endure.
She wished that she could read, and thus relieve
the continued nightmare.

Far into the night she would sit, waiting the
return of Mr. Mourn, about whom nothing was
certain but his terrible moods of violence. Sitting
there alone in the parlour she would read the
trend of local events in the footsteps of the neighbours passing; for when Jessica came up from
the bowels of Kent Street she, unknowing,
brought with her a divination and a philosophy
wrought in the echo of footsteps.

For so many years the world had walked overhead and rattled the gratings as it passed down
Kent Street, and in the long silences of the basement she had become acutely sensitive to the
language of footsteps passing.

The Past only was real, and more and more
she came to live in the Past.

She filled the little parlour with emblems of
Kent Street: there was the leather sofa whose
inward parts came out piece by piece leaving
the surface undulating, but in the course of
time, and fortified by her strong sense of past
associations, Jessica learned to " get between the
springs " of the sofa for such sleep as she took.

The sofa had belonged to Jessica's mother who received it at the hands of 'Erb Roper, last of the Roper line, a grim relic embodying for me the dire history of the Roper clan as I had heard it from Jessica.

On the mantelpiece was the oddest collection of inflexible countenances in china and, sentinel at each end, two large glass vases encasing some dyed grass that had belonged to her mother—time-defying, shrill green as ever.

On Saturdays I dusted the ornaments and never moved the two glass vases containing the artificial grass.

Jessica rarely mentioned the deceased Mr. Mourn, and when she did speak of him, she employed that restraint she strongly felt was due to the dead—and always mentioned his ability to read and write. . . .

With her attachment to the Past, Jessica cherished a touching faith in " Them what's above," to whom she unreservedly committed the griefs and disasters of Jipping Street that it was in her large heart to contain but beyond her power to repair. She drew trouble to her like a magnet; everyone sent for Jessica Mourn. She watched by the dying; she laid out the dead:

43

these melancholy tasks were her daily portion. The excursions she made beyond the confines of Jipping Street were invariably undertaken to comfort the afflicted. Once or twice I accompanied her on these journeys.

I remember how one day she took me to see Miss Le Grand, who was in the workhouse.

It was Sunday afternoon, for visitors to the workhouse were only permitted on Sunday afternoons. We took with us a small bag of peppermint drops, and I carried them. In summer Jessica took acid drops for Miss Le Grand, which tasted tartly and were said to refresh the mouth.

It was the first Sunday in December; an ominous gloom hung from the sky; the wind met us harshly at each corner and found every half-dried spot on my face, which had been washed before we started and, in the hurry and excitement, improperly dried, so that soon my forehead seemed linked to my chin in a stinging smart.

We kept silent on the way so that we should not take cold " through the mouth "; and I fell to thinking of Miss Le Grand whom Jessica never mentioned without saying that she was a " born lady," and her voice would reach low in

44

a reverent hush. I knew that Miss Le Grand once lived in the back room next to Jessica, and was an old lady who wore white caps and " kept herself to herself."

Through the workhouse gates we went, down a long stone corridor, which had walls of green bricks, glazed and clammy to the touch. Soon we found ourselves in a room of bewildering space; it seemed at first that the space had swallowed everything else, but presently I picked out little black objects huddled together in regular intervals about the walls; and I saw that there were forms to sit on round the room, and there were texts on the walls, in such dressy letters that it was not easy to read them. The place filled me with a sickening fear—confused, inarticulate—and I clutched at Jessica's shawl as if she, too, would be swallowed up in so much space, or succumb to the intangible but no less chilly and hateful influences that seemed to brood over everything.

I smelled the smell of very washed old ladies, a dry sad smell mixed up with the smell of newly washed clothes, not put out to air.

The room was barrenly without corner or recess—so clean that the east wind might have

45

swept bleakly through it just before we came; bleak and barren the room was, and at first sight the old ladies seemed but part of its bleak barrenness: cruelly clean and garnished, dressed uniformly in dark grey frocks which buttoned down the front and were stiffly voluminous, which served to mark and heighten their lean shrivelled bodies.

Soon Miss Le Grand had found us, and in the first flush of the meeting Jessica had forgotten me, and I watched Miss Le Grand's courtly reception crumble before Jessica's emotional embrace; but in a moment Miss Le Grand had remembered herself, and composedly turned to receive me, while the tears welled up in Jessica's eyes and she wept without restraint. I wanted to weep with Jessica, but the sight of Miss Le Grand stayed my tears.

She had white hair drawn tightly from the face and leaving the brow fully revealed, and it was a little thinned so that you could see the pinkish scalp. She had eyes of a dissolving blue, infinitely puckered about their corners, connecting with the lines in her face and there losing themselves in her cheeks: they crossed and re-crossed in her peaky chin.

46

Her features were clear-cut like a cameo; eyes, nose, chin, as it were, fixed questioningly on something beyond, ahead. Nervous little hands she had that did not tremble, but you scarcely wanted to touch them for fear of pressing too much on the blue veins. There was a hurry in her step; her manner was quaintly brisk and authoritative; she spoke incisively and, most of all when she spoke, you knew why Jessica always talked of her as a " lady." And I wished that Jessica would not cry, for there was that in Miss Le Grand's manner which seemed not to call for tears.

We three sat on a form, Miss Le Grand seeking out the most solitary place, and they fell to talking about the workhouse.

Miss Le Grand spoke of the uninterrupted days and the long nights in the workhouse; of the monotony so sustained that it defied the times of the day, no less than the seasons of the year—she could not tell, she said, whether it was Monday or Thursday.

Soon the workhouse bell clanged to tell us to leave. Miss Le Grand saw us to the door and smiled sweetly at me when I handed her the peppermint drops. Jessica could not speak, for her eyes were filled with tears, and very red from the tears that she had shed.

Down the corridor we looked back and waved at Miss Le Grand; and now in the street we hardly noticed the gloom or the freezing cold, for our thoughts were full of Miss Le Grand.

. . . . . . . .

One day it came to me strong and clear—the end of all desires, the longing beneath all longing; and there shaped in my dreams a little room with white walls, clean white-washed walls, and bare floor boards, set far away on the brow of a hill I had never seen, remote, inaccessible. Swirling, fugitive at the foot of the hill, the world pressed on—Jipping Street.

In the centre of the room was a square, solid, white deal table, for scrubbing; there was a chair I could scrub and, in magnificent array about the room, the bookshelves I myself had builded supporting the books I had most strangely become possessed of; and in the room there dwelt peace and cleanness in perfect accord and sanctity.

I was nearly twelve. How I sickened of people; loathing them! From morning until night, and again in the morning: people, people, in travail with their insufferable burdens. They toiled all day as I toiled, and felt about them the unseen, unsubstantial chains of a slavery too real for sight and substance, but biting into the soul.

I shrank from them because they scattered and refuted my dreams, with their tired eyes and indomitable endurance: subtle, insidious enemies of revolt, with their forlorn, wooden acceptance of the intolerable burden of life in Jipping Street. Going on and on from the beginning to the end; from the sticky, shiny, smelling perambulator—with a teat stuffed in the mouth to keep you quiet—to the grave or, like Miss Le Grand, to the workhouse.

There were, however, escapes—compensations like old "Blast-the-Wax," who mended boots in a small narrow shop off the stables fronting Jipping Street, and had a habit of swearing aloud to himself when the wax would not stick on the sides of the new soles; for which reason we children called him "Blast-the-Wax," and, to his horror and disgust, he came to be known by this name through the neighbourhood. Then there was Albert, the basket-maker, who had a shed in Ben Rents.

" Blast-the-Wax " it was who gave me my earliest lessons in politics. He was a disciple of Marx, and a firm reader of Mr. Blatchford. Together we read *Merrie England*, and a periodical called the *Clarion*. Furthermore, from sitting often in his shop I learned to mend my own boots and my mother's boots.

" Blast-the-Wax " seemed to live with a consuming anger, and our visits together were much interrupted by a flow of unseemly language if he should miss the nail and hit his finger with the hammer, or if, as more commonly happened, the wax melted too quickly or did not melt soon enough.

There was, too, a singular miserliness in his character, and I recall how once he was ill and Jessica came to " look-in " on him with her Pharmacopœia (inherited from her mother and carried in her infallible memory).

" You look noo-monia," said Jessica sadly.

" I've got pains all over," said " Blast-the-Wax." "First they're here, then they're there."

" Why don't you get yourself a nice noo laid egg? " said Jessica.

" Can't afford it," growled " Blast-the-Wax."

" P'r'aps, then," said Jessica (I shall never forget the quiet scorn in her tones), " you can manage a shop egg! " (shop eggs being one farthing cheaper than eggs newly laid).

Albert, the basket-maker, was cast in a more generous hue, and although he shared the political views of " Blast-the-Wax " (I was not old enough to be aware of the subtle differences which, no doubt, existed), he brought more of intellect and less of passion into the propagation of his social theories.

Albert was not accepted with that easy casualness with which " Blast-the-Wax," for example, was accepted. People avoided his shed, and he made no social overtures. Even my mother disliked him, and said that she would " brain " me if she caught me there; and as the feeling in the neighbourhood against him increased, I the more passionately espoused his cause. It offended my sense of justice and of the proper that Albert should be treated like a pariah; for even my mother admitted that he had " done no one no wrong " as far as she knew, but that it was for the looks of him, and what he might do, that people punished him.

I continued to sit in Albert's shed and soak his willow sticks in the reeking tank he kept for this purpose, and saw no wrong in Albert, and knew no fear. Albert had travelled much on the earth's spaces, and told me stories of black men who put white-hot pokers in their mouths " without turning a hair "; and how once he was nearly drowned in the Caribbean sea, being saved in the nick of time but not before he had tasted the sensations of death, and, said he, " In a moment of time I seemed to re-live the whole of my past life."

Albert's stories of adventure were only exceeded by his powers as a narrator. I have never met his equal. With infinite leisureliness he would proceed with the story, marking the pregnant parts with long pauses in which your excitement and eagerness reached fever point. Then Albert would carefully spit across the shed, wipe his mouth, and resume the thread of his narrative.

One day Albert's shed did not open its doors. A week later we heard that he was in prison. He had slit the throat of a little girl in Clapham. My mother said " What did I tell you! " I was not so much frightened by the news as I was utterly astonished and miserable. I simply could not think of Albert in that connection.

Meanwhile we lived in our rooms at the hospital end of Jipping Street, and mother went out to scrub in the morning and we took in washing to occupy the afternoons and evenings, and I sat in Jessica's parlour, or slid unseen round the gates of the stable in Jipping Street and climbed to the top of the pantechnicon that was housed there, and hid myself from everyone among the sacks and shavings. In this solitude a more benevolent spirit would well up in me, and quiet the turmoil within; and I dreamed my dreams.

# III

# ACROSS LONDON BRIDGE

# I I I

I GOT up in the mornings, and each fresh morning there was a quality of eager promise in the day before me. Sitting on the canal steps, I could quietly snatch at the day before it was astir.

Life was vigorous, unrelenting; the multitude of odd jobs I performed was matched only by their singular unremunerativeness. Every penny weighed. I have the memory of winter mornings before the dawn, that time of day when the dark seems most improper and out of place—desolating mornings when the cold does not bite and sting, but damply enwraps you with a leech-like embrace.

We had to rise early for a place in the wood-line, and vividly I recall in those first frigid moments greeting the dawn with querulous tears seemingly frozen under the eyelids (but keeping the eyes open); the blind groping after clothes, and the growing sense of the urgency of the occasion, for wood we had to get.

57

Again, in the street to be frozen to all but the sense of utter desolation. I would make a muff of my wood-sack to keep my hands warm, and from some less frozen spot inside my head I directed the speed and motion of my feet: my legs I could not feel from the knee down.

The wood-yard was only half a mile away, but on winter mornings it seemed an endless stretch in Greenland.

We huddled close together in the wood-line to keep each other warm. At six o'clock the coffee-shop opposite opened, and we smelled the smell of kippers frying, and bloaters—warm, human smells, to increase our sense of the long, long waiting.

Through the windows of the coffee-shop we beheld a scene of infinite unrest as the proprietor of the " Anchor " rattled the mugs in place, restored the upturned forms and tables, blew out his cheeks, tied the strings of his dirty white apron with the air of a man who has all to hope and nothing to fear—certainly not the hunger we suffered.

Presently the customers came, shadowy figures out of the gloom, and slowly the steam from the tea-urn rose sheer up the front of the window, dissolved and gathered in little streams that fell irregularly down the face of the window as sheet after sheet of steam rose up the surface of the glass, sealing and re-sealing the privacy within, leaving us to imaginings that drew down the face and made more hollow the stomach.

At last the wood-yard opened to the queue of cramped mutes that we by this time had become; and I remember with what an inscrutable countenance the yard boss finally dealt out the wood—a figure to thrill our frozen limbs with fear and awe. Yet, as one's turn came, one seemed to read into his stern face a certain kindliness, to feel an outrush of gratitude as chump displaced chump in the sack, aimed by this compassionate Olympian who never once relaxed his features nor opened his mouth, except to say at intervals: " Get a move on, stiff guts! " Stiff we were.

On Saturdays I sold salt with Mrs. Bennett who lived in Jipping Street and clandestinely stabled in her backyard a donkey, Dolphus, a creature of most mournful mien; and Mrs. Bennett long continued her illegal practice of stabling Dolphus in the backyard, because the neighbours feared her intimidating person even more than they resented the hoarse notes of

Dolphus which broke out regularly at midnight and with the dawn.

There were nights when I went out with Blind Dan, who played a harmonium outside the public-houses, when the spirit moved him and it was necessary to augment the meagre relief from the parish—three shillings and sixpence a week.

I sang sentimental songs which Dan taught me on the harmonium, and for the many lapses in the words of the songs (Dan's memory was weak) I atoned by drawing out the more pathetic notes; and in time I grew to fit to the tunes words and lines of my own creation.

Dan carried the harmonium from public-house to public-house; I collected coppers after each "turn," in a green baize bag which, strictly speaking, belonged to the mission hall.

The entertainment we furnished was not too varied: "Robert Emmett" I sang, and "Eileen Alannah," and a song with seventeen verses which told of the rise and fall of a servant girl, and her subsequent death by drowning. I omitted some of the verses, but I never failed to give "lung" to the stanza which asked if she "was pushed, or did she fall in?"

My voice grew hoarse on these excursions, but I preferred to sing songs with Blind Dan than to sell salt with Mrs. Bennett. Also my emotions were moved by the pathos of the songs we sang, the melancholy burden of the words. Often I would weep as I sang, weep delicious tears.

I made myself of use to Nellie the barmaid in the " World On Its Toes." I fetched her Dutch cheese for the bar, which she cut up and sold in penny pieces; I ran for her hairpins which she used in great quantities, and from time to time I renewed the sawdust on the bar floors, the " Private " bar and the bar for " Jugs and Bottles."

Nellie was very kind to children and much given to " complaints," which meant frequent excursions to the hospital on the ancient site, and much talk over the bar of the " World On Its Toes," where everyone sympathised with Nellie.

On these excursions to the hospital I was commissioned to attend with her, and after she had been " seen " by the doctor, I waited more hours at the hospital dispensary for her medicine and bandages and ointments.

At the hospital and over the bar of the " World
On Its Toes " I learned of many matters that are
not generally included in the instruction of the
young.

On the whole I was not unpopular in Jipping
Street. Nellie the barmaid approved my serious
attitude to life and discussed with me at much
length problems of the bar, and the ravages, no
less than the complexities, of her diseases, as if
I had grown to the understanding of mature
years.

Mrs. Moody, for whom, among others, my
mother washed, once called me " intelligent,"
and this flattered my pride for many weeks.
The compliment was occasioned on an evening
when I sat with her round her fireside awaiting
the arrival of " Mr. Moody," who was to
pay me the washing money. There was, I had
long observed, more than one Mr. Moody, and
this information I had imparted to my mother,
who turned up her nose and spat on the wash-
house floor to convey to me her inexpressible
contempt for the impecunious, harassed, but
none the less charming Mrs. Moody.

As we waited, Mrs. Moody hung the washing
round the fire to air. On the hob a kettle boiled,

and I noticed that the steam from the kettle, dispersing in particular on a pair of pants, was intent on undoing all the " airing," whereupon I respectfully drew Mrs. Moody's attention to this state of affairs, while Mrs. Moody stood aghast at the acuteness of my observation and my penetrating intelligence.

I was serious, intelligent—I utterly accepted the verdict of Mrs. Moody—also I was willing, and God knows the neighbours in Jipping Street exercised my willingness. I assiduously kept myself in mind of these talents and virtues, and this compensated me in some measure for my ever-present consciousness of my physical deficiencies.

I had a rather full mouth, and sometimes the kids in Jipping Street called me " Nigger Lips." My mother said, however, that it was only that my top lip was where my bottom lip should be. My nose was small, and turned upwards. " That," said mother drily, " is all because I cuddled you too close to my breast when you were a baby." I remember that she was given to wiping my nose frequently on the coarse apron she wore at the wash-tub. I had dark brown hair, curly, and always entangled. My mother straightened out the tangles with an iron comb, a horse comb I found in the stables. This was almost as painful as having my nose wiped on the coarse apron.

The size of my head seemed definitely out of proportion to the shape of my body; and the cast-off clothing I wore did not atone for my lack of form, nor distract from the disproportion of my head to the rest of my person, and while my clothes never improved, my sensitiveness was never diminished. I suffered anguish on account of my looks and my person; but this I kept profoundly secret.

IV

LIL

# I V

WHEN I consider how my days were spent before I went out from Jipping Street to work, it seems odd that the change should have assumed the tragic proportions it did assume, filling my days with a haunting fear, conjuring up in my imagination the most menacing prospects. I shuddered at the very thought of it, while resigning myself to the inevitable; for I was nearly thirteen, and as long as I could remember I had been disciplined to the prospect of earning my living in the world outside of Jipping Street. Moreover, what was obvious to me, though utterly without comfort, was the fact that all the other girls and boys in Jipping Street did, in the order of things, go out to work at the earliest possible moment. They took on a new way of looking at life, and put away childish things.

Whenever I thought of my fate, now imminent, the future stretched out before me black and horrible. I was filled with alarms, and I could no longer dream my dreams in the face of this reality. Impatient as I was of the helplessness, the exposure of childhood, now that the time was approaching to put it away for ever, I wept unavailing tears, and in an agony of emotion formed desperate projects of escape—wild, impossible escape.

The days sped past on the wings of fear: I feared being out of the reach of my mother's strong presence; I saw clear visions of a new slavery, and feared it; I was afraid of the unknown I was about to face.

So I shed my unavailing tears, and bemoaned my cruel fate, and trembled for the unknown horror before me, and sure as Fate the day dawned when, armoured against hunger with four slices of bread and dripping, fortified by a few curt words from my mother, I walked down Jipping Street over the interminable London Bridge in a pair of hockey boots my mother had picked up cheap on a stall.

I sickeningly remember those hockey boots, associated as they are with the anguish of first going out to work. They had the oddest bumps on the soles and on the ankles, and I recall how,

with a sullen defiance bred in the pride of being
about to go to work, I said:

"I won't wear boots with bumps all over them."

"Mind you don't get a bloody bump some-
where else," said mother; and all the world
seemed to look at my feet from Jipping Street to
Aldersgate Street.

"I've got weak ankles," I said, when people
asked me about the bumps; and I suffered a
cringing shame that my boots should be so
foolishly unlike the boots that other people wore.

I remember little of those first reluctant
contributions I made to the world on the far
side of London Bridge, for all other memories
are cast over and obscured in the dull aching
memory of the sheer physical tiredness I grew
to know—a tiredness which paralysed all thought
and feeling.

Daily I walked from Jipping Street across the
bridge to the Monument, and from the Monument to St. Paul's, losing myself in the labyrinth
of streets behind the cathedral, until I came to
Jewin Street by way of Aldersgate. I retraced
my steps at night with less spirit, taking a rest
on the steps of St. Paul's, and again a rest at the
foot of the Monument. I took my boots off on

the curb of London Bridge, for in addition to the unnecessary bumps on my hockey boots, they were a size too small, and at night, coming over London Bridge, it was like seven thousand red devils pricking, pinching, squeezing my feet until they felt like a long crease of red-hot fire. So I sat on the curb and took them off, and walked the rest of the way to Jipping Street with my boots in my hand.

My duties in Jewin Street began promptly at eight o'clock. For this I rose at six, left Jipping Street at seven, and in unwise fashion I expended my day's energy before I reached Jewin Street raging against the Fates, and conceiving plans for wild, impossible escape.

All of which succeeded only in making me very hungry, and often, by the time I reached St. Paul's, I made inroads on the bread and dripping I carried for my lunch. Sometimes I fed the pigeons.

Our business in Jewin Street was the manufacture of men's collars, and I began my day dismantling the coverings from the machines at which the women sat—one hundred odd coverings, which made the room look strangely like a morgue overflowing with white-clad corpses.

At eleven, at one o'clock, and again in the afternoon at four, I faithfully carried a long broom-handle filled with beer cans to the " Welcome," where my cans were filled with ha'p'orths of tea, coffee, cocoa, for the women who needed these beverages. At one o'clock, in addition to drink, I bought innumerable ha'p'orths of cheese, pickles, bread, and, for the more prosperous ones, two pen'orth of steak, or bacon—cut with a knife that had lain near the ham!

I grew expert in balancing the cans on my broom-handle, and at sneaking sips of cocoa or tea out of the cans as I walked up the dark stairs to the machine-room. Also, I picked at the cheese and contented myself with smelling the bacon cut with a hammy knife, and imagining my emotions on first eating such delicacies.

When the women had departed, after 7.30, I proceeded about my melancholy finishing touches to the work-room. I put each machine to bed in its voluminous nightgown, and swept up the dirt from the floor, banging the broom about within an inch of its life to relieve my feelings, for I was so tired by this time that I could only weep impotently as I swept, and swallow more dust than could possibly have been good for me.

The tiredness, the sheer physical exhaustion that came upon me at this time of the day is my most enduring memory. I could have slept as I stood. To this day I cannot look at Jewin Street without being overwhelmed with the tiredness I there knew—an aching tiredness, drawn out by the knowledge of a to-morrow which would surely bring with it the same inexpressible fatigue.

Then, like a ray of light from heaven, shining a little unsteadily and with a preternatural brightness, Lil came into my life; and I have preserved her memory fragrant, to relieve those early days of grey foreboding, but without the power to stay her laughter or dim the light of her eyes. I see her most clearly in obscurest settings which, without her face and the sound of her laughter, leave only a dull sense of inexorable wrong.

Lil came from Ben Rents to stitch buttons in the Jewin Street factory—Ben Rents which reared its tenements by the side of the jam factory at the back of Jipping Street; and she succeeded, without displacing, Jessica in my devotions and allegiance.

72

To come from Jessica to Lil was like passing
from deep shades to the irresistible sunshine, a
little garish and tinselled, leaving you to wonder,
to be uncertain. It was as if the gods had be-
stowed on her the gift of unending laughter,
while Life, that appeared so menacing in Jipping
Street, looked on grimly and half concealed the
mortal thrust.

People shook their heads and said " No good
will come of Lil Reeds," and watched her down
the street when she seemed to dance as she
walked, and laughter looked out even from the
tip of her high-heeled button boots, impatient
of the pavement.

She smiled at the neighbours as she passed
down Jipping Street.

One thinks of her smile, the laughing movement of her walk, the upward fling of her head,
for these things were Lil; and of the frail body
(like a ha'p'orth of Gawd 'elp us, they said at the
factory) mortgaged by a quenchless spirit; of
the little expediencies so much a part of her:
how she would, as if by magic, inform her
colourless face and pale lips with a glowing
health through the medium of a penny dictionary,
from whose red-covered back she stole, with a

73

lick of the tongue, the outward look of health. Or how with consummate art she toned its first rude redness with a little whitewash rubbed off the wall!

Lil lived with her father in two rooms on the second floor of one of the tenements in Ben Rents, and ever since she was small her mother had lived away from them.

Her father worked at night, printing newspapers, and he slept most of the day. I saw him once—a little wizened man, with a leaden-hued face from working all night under brilliant arc lights in the printing works, Lil said; he had a sly, meaning half-grin on his face, and lecherous eyes which blinked in the light of day to which he was by now almost a stranger.

Once, too, I saw her mother, on a night when we came home together from Jewin Street and found her lying at the foot of the tenement stone stairs with her head cut open. We took her to the hospital on the ancient site. . . .

Sometimes, at the end of the long day, I used to wonder if it would be possible to walk home without Lil dancing along by the side of me, now singing, now laughing—full of an uncontainable thrill in living. She seemed removed from all the things that made the days to be dreaded—tiredness, feet that did not fit easily into the second-hand boots picked up cheap on a stall. She seemed removed even from the pangs of hunger. Life presented to her no questions, no problems, no sadness; and people looked on her with envy, and suspicion.

Something not human looked out from her eyes —it was too bright a light, and without the colour she borrowed from the penny dictionaries her face was ashen and grey—grey face, eyes brimming over with dancing lights: it made you catch your breath and wonder; and in a moment the wonder was lost in the sound of her laughter. . . .

She was nineteen at this time, I was still a long way from fourteen, and I gladly undertook the task of waking her in the mornings in time for work. Otherwise she would sleep till noon. I made her breakfast tea, which she drank while she dressed, and I cut her a slice of bread, which she ate as we hurried to work over London Bridge, in the intervals of putting her hat straight and attending to other parts of her dressing passed over in the hurry.

I respected her age and maturity and she laughed, not unkindly, at my solemnities. In spite of the contrast between our ages and the oppositeness of our dispositions, we achieved a firm friendship, expressed on my side by uncritical admiration, unquestioning trust, and an inordinate desire to serve her.

Lil accepted admiration as her natural portion in life, and I also grew to accept the numbers of young bloods in the neighbourhood who fought over her and, to ease the sorrows she caused them, drank themselves drunk in the " World On Its Toes " until closing time, when they would engage in recriminations and pleadings on her doorstep in Ben Rents far into the night.

They cultivated me as a means of approach to Lil. I carried to her their favours, and similarly I was the vehicle of their threats, while Lil, impervious to threats and to favours, continued to glow for them and artfully distribute her attentions.

My continued happiness was in walking with Lil to work, and walking home from work with Lil. Nightly I would sit in Ben Rents and watch her dress for the pleasures before her : a music-hall in the London Road, the theatre at the Elephant, with sometimes a fish supper to precede or to conclude the evening's entertainment. Many

were the nights brought to an exciting close by
some young man who awaited Lil in Ben Rents
to chastise her for duping him on the outing, for
Lil had no conscience in these matters; and the
young man would forlornly await her by the
hospital end of Jipping Street, or at the foot of
London Bridge, while Lil was disappearing
down the Borough with another of her sudden
choice and liking.

I think at this moment of the pair of button
boots she once bought me in order to see me
in boots that came near to the size of my feet.
They were of patent leather, with buttons of
a startlingly bright colour, stretching to my
shins and above them; and I know that Lil
saved for many weeks to get them. We bought
them in Brick Lane one lunch time, and Lil
haggled so long over the purchase that we were
very late in getting back to the factory in Jewin
Street.

I know that I took almost as much pride and
pleasure in wearing these boots as I took in
buying for Lil, for a few pence, a back comb for
her birthday—a bright, glittering, incredible
bauble set with two angels recumbent on the
frame of the comb; Lil had a taste for arresting

77

ornaments. And though the boots soon shed their patent and their buttons, and I lost one of the high heels, and the angels recumbent on Lil's back comb lost all shape and seemliness as the stones fell away one after another, and the teeth came out until there were left only two teeth, it did not diminish our pride and thrill in these possessions.

People hinted at the wildest irregularities, and attributed them to Lil; and now when I think of it I see that she was not much concerned with the moral aspect of life or her own pleasures; but she smiled at the women when she sailed through the factory, and people smiled back at her, for Lil was irresistible.

She brought to us all the sun and the stars of another world, and its laughter.

Lil was twenty when the light went out from her eyes and we heard her voice no more.

A little white box, trimmed with fancy paper, —like the paper on which stood the wedding cakes at the pastry shop in the Borough—supported by a trestle, stood at the foot of the bed: in it was Lil's baby, two days old.

It was hot, swooning hot in the bedroom, as if every breath of air was oppressed by the coming of death, and suddenly a great change seemed to come over all the room: the walls went grey and dirty; the lace curtains at the window became stringy, lank, torn and indescribably miserable looking. The room took on a sordidness that sent a shiver through my soul— the very room in which I had so often watched Lil fluff her hair and steal her look of health from the red-covered back of a penny dictionary, and shed my cares in the sound of her laughter.

Jessica laid out the body reverently, and we could not help remembering that Lil was fond of saying, in the days when she little dreamed of death, that she must be well wrapped up on her last journey to prevent the " maggots taking liberties " with her.

Well wrapped up she was, too, and " going decent," as Jessica felt that one should go.

I went to the funeral on Jessica's lap, in the one carriage that followed the hearse to Forest Hill. And I remember, in a mist of tears, the crowds in Ben Rents; horses pawing the ground; children pawing the horses; the stuffy black carriage; the clay-sodden ground of the cemetery, and the inexpressibly bleak church, where a surpliced figure obscurely muttered the burial service; and in the deeply dug, sodden clay we buried the sun and stars of another world—and its laughter.

# V

## LIFE THAT GOES ON!

# V

In my grief for the death of Lil I saw that the dreams of childhood also were gone, those visions of an impossible future that I saw sitting on the canal steps before the day was begun— impossible dreams, more real and sustaining than anything in life, bringing more consolation. In losing Lil I saw that my dreams had fled before the realities of earning a living, for in the laughter of Lil's presence one could put away dreams. Now there was left only the Future—the hollow, hateful years, without dreams, without end.

Bleak, unheeding world! Life that goes on! So I ran my errands all day, and although I frequently changed my job, I continued to run errands to all parts of the City. By the end of the year my wages had been raised from four to five shillings a week, and I conceived a dread and distaste for the City of London, within the borders of Ludgate Hill and the Monument, that will last to the end of my days.

Hollow, hateful years! I shrink even now from looking back at them, the hateful years, crowding life into an hour of the day before seven, when I left Jipping Street, and could sit alone and flavour the day before the day was astir.

I had lost my dreams and I grew away from the people in Jipping Street who consoled my childhood, because they accepted without question, although with eternal complaint, a state of things that I found intolerable. I could not reconcile myself; I was filled with unrest; I questioned and criticised; I raged and rebelled and knew that in acceptance came a measure of peace, only I could not pay the price of such peace. Some uncontainable force spurred me on and on to where I knew not, nor to what end.

I accustomed myself to hunger and that tiredness which takes away all sense of feeling; only, I could not accept; I could not accustom myself to acceptance. I formed wild plans of escape, and one morning, early, with two shillings I had laboriously saved, I took an excursion ticket to Southend instead of going to work.

I arrived on the sandless beach of Southend with a stockinette bathing costume and four slices of bread and dripping—and that calm which comes to the desperate when they have made a last gesture. I bought some cockles, and these I ate with my bread and dripping. I coveted an ice-cream cornet for my dessert, but I recalled Jessica telling me of a girl who ate ice-cream after having eaten winkles, and the ice froze the winkles, said Jessica, and the girl died a painful death.

For a long time I sat on the beach, even till the sun slipped down behind the horizon in slow passages of red flame, shot with purple, and changing to a myriad-shaded pearl, as the white clouds passed and re-passed over the ball of flame.

The night came on, and like a moth drawn to the brightest light I hovered about the minstrels who made entertainment for the trippers under a great canvas tent. In time I found my way to the back of the naphtha-lit theatre, where I lay flat on my chest and pushed my head under the canvas and saw almost as much as if I had paid my money at the entrance.

Presently I became aware that the entertainment was drawing to a close. The tent was emptying. Soon it was altogether empty, and the lights went out; and then it was I became conscious of an insistent and nagging pain in my stomach, which I at once attributed to the cockles and which was probably due to the damp ground on which I had been lying. I thought of the girl who died a painful death, and even the certain knowledge that I had abstained from ice-cream for at least two hours after my lunch did not greatly comfort me. I was plunged in dismal reflection.

I felt miserable—and horribly alone. Now the streets were almost deserted, and I was tired and cold and still clinging to the stockinette bathing costume I had brought down with my bread and dripping, and which I had dipped in the water, for it seemed to me absurd to be nursing a dry bathing costume, and I disliked the idea of bathing myself in the water.

In the morning, when I had arrived in the full glare of the sun, I had resolved to pass my nights on the beach. Now I wandered down the beach, but there was no sun, it was bitterly cold. I was frightened by the roar of the sea. I had never heard such sounds before.

I hastened from the beach.

I thought of throwing myself on the mercies

86

of a policeman, but I suppressed the temptation. I had been brought up with a healthy dislike of policemen.

I continued disconsolately to wander round and round the town. I fell to weeping. There seemed nothing else to do. Everything was so overwhelmingly strange, and I had not been out of London before. I wept more from the cold and strangeness than in actual fear, and at last, wiping my eyes on the damp swimming costume, I accosted a lady hurrying along the High Street.

Could she tell me where I might sleep the night? I told her a lie. I came for the day, I said, and now I had lost the last train home.

She was very kind. She knew where I could sleep, she said, and together we hastened down the High Street, striking off into a road of suburban houses with shrubberies in the front gardens. Near the end of the road we paused, and I followed her into the front gate of a large house. A nun opened the door to us.

By this time I was so tired that I could not attend to what was happening; but I remember that the nun led me up the stairs to a bedroom, and on the landing outside the door hung my bathing costume to dry.

87

I thereupon fell into a profound sleep, and was incontinently wakened the next morning by another nun who spoke softly and made me tea and gave me bread and butter to eat. Then she led me to the railway station where, at 6.30 a.m., she packed me into the first train for Fenchurch Street.

# VI

# REBELLION

# V I

It was as if the time had definitely come when I must take hold of the world and deal with it; and after long brooding and much painful cogitation, in a boldness bred of despair, I pinned my hair up at the back and presented myself at a factory near Jipping Street as a person much older than I was. With the utmost effrontery I offered myself as a skilled worker.

When I had run errands in the factory I had watched the women working at their machines, and on one or two occasions I had clandestinely worked the machines before I put them away in their nightgowns. On this precarious basis I thought to take on the status—and the wages—of a grown woman.

The gods, in the persons of the women who sat immediately near me in the factory, befriended me, and, strange to say, I managed to keep my new job and effect the giddy elevation in my wages from five shillings to fifteen shillings a week. Oh then for weeks I walked on air!

Twelve hours a day, with a reluctant break for dinner and for tea, I glued my eyes to the machine in a fever of longing to do my best while apprehending in every footstep, every shadow across my work table, the approach of the forewoman come to strip me of my pretences and order me out of the factory. A week passed before I became aware even of the room in which I worked, or the noise of the machinery, which seemed to deafen the ears and stupefy the senses. When the machinery paused for the dinner hour and for tea, it was as if the hand of death had fallen over all the world, the hush was so instant, so awe-full. And Heaven alone can know how terrified I was at the sight of the forewoman, who, with the face of Cerberus black as night, brooding at the door of hell, stood aloof and surveyed the scene of our endeavours.

In Jipping Street the change in my status was swift—marvellous. My mother was able to give up taking in washing, and now devoted her afternoons tending and resting the wounds of the varicose veins she had developed in years of standing at the wet wash-tub and rising prematurely from childbirths casually attended. Two afternoons she visited the hospital on the ancient

site at the far end of Jipping Street, where she
waited hours for a few moments' attendance
from the overworked doctors, and brought away
with her fresh bandages and liniment and ointments for her dreadful wounds.

I got me a room, a back room, opposite the
hospital in the house of one Mrs. Perks, who
loaned out money in the neighbourhood for the
sum of one penny interest in the shilling per
week. My landlady, the moneylender, was
tolerably clean, and she kept her front door
closed. She did not live on the pavement outside
her house as did most of the women in Jipping
Street, from the wise conviction, no doubt, that
by keeping herself aloof she could the better
exact her pound of flesh from the neighbours in
Jipping Street who borrowed from her on
Monday and repaid the debt on Saturday with
a tedious regularity.

In time I came to feel at ease in the grown
company of the women in the factory, and I
learned out of their experience, in the language
they spoke one to another, of the things I had
not already learned about the secrets of men and
women at night, and the mysteries of sex that I
had seen, as a child, prowling down the canal

bank in the dark—furtive, sly, silent, wrapped in an inexpressible and fearful ugliness from which I by early training shrank and covered my face, for my mother included in her singular and strong character a repugnance for all irregularities—a harsh, uncompromising puritanism which would not permit even of a lewdness in our hearing. She never spoke to us of this matter on which she had taken so unbending a stand, and no words could have spoken more clearly to us than her consistent attitude.

Outside of our—in this respect—austere home we became unavoidably acquainted with the passions of men and women as we saw them at the closing time of the " World On Its Toes," in meaning looks and leering winks, and heard the language of sex, reeking hotly of beer and whiskey, expressed in phrases and words that smote the ear and seared into the soul.

Passionately, obscurely, sex came to mean for me all that was horrible and revolting, all that was inexpressibly ugly; and only a little less strong than my horror was my curiosity. I listened as a child to the whispered meaning talk of the women in Jipping Street, standing at their front doors. I knew at a delicate age the significance of the words and looks they used one to another in their street quarrels, and in the quarrels of the men and women, which were continual.

We children talked in the gutter of the processes of creation as, luridly, we knew them; and the spectacle of a pregnant woman held no secrets for us, nor reverence, as we exchanged knowing winks and remarks picked up outside the " World On Its Toes," and from the lips of those mothers and fathers who, while they encouraged and laughed at the precocious chatter of babes scarcely out of arms mouthing some foul obscenity, boxed our ears when we grew a little older for repeating so faithfully their own language. The fact of motherhood awakened in me only emotions of disgust and recoiling.

An incident remains with me from these encounters as a child in Jipping Street. Mrs. Murphy's eldest daughter, Kate, had a large head and a stupid face. " Crazy Kate " we called her. My mother said her head grew instead of her brain, and I accepted this explanation while refusing to accept Crazy, whom I loathed.

Crazy Kate seemed to mind all the babies in Jipping Street in the intervals of having fits, which were preceded by spasms of ungovernable rage. Once Crazy killed all the pigeons in Mrs. Bennet's backyard—strangled them.

My mother and Mrs. Murphy were discussing Crazy, who had that day been taken to see a doctor in the hospital on the ancient site. The conversation flowed on in low, pregnant whispers. I listened, unseen, outside the kitchen door.

"And the doctor said, he says, ' What was your husband before Crazy was born? '

" Says I, 'A soldier, I says. In India.'

" ' Humph,' says the doctor. He says, ' Enough to explain all of little Crazy.' "

There was a pause, a long, throbbing, terrible pause. I strained my ear at the crack of the door.

"What do *you* make of it?" asked Mrs. Murphy of my mother, before she gave herself over to a fit of weeping.

I remember my mother's bitter retort: "We can't make nothing about them sort of things. Pity you didn't turn over on Crazy when she was born. Saved yourself a lot of trouble."

Then, with a more deadly tinge to her voice, " Men must have their little pleasures."

I shivered. Ran wildly out into Jipping Street. I felt I knew what they were saying, but I could not understand.

Next day I played marbles with Crazy, and wiped her nose when it needed wiping, instead of turning away sick.

I became more fully informed at the factory, but my disgust and fear were hardly diminished, and I came more and more to marvel at the incredible acceptance of these women of the endless sufferings that came to them from experiences which, while they were common and conventional, like eating and growing older and getting into debt on Monday and repaying the loans on Saturday, gave them so little pleasure, so little joy.

I observed, painfully, that while their conversation was full of complaint and revolt, it seemed strangely to leave their conduct unaffected, and they produced children, and diseases, and " women's complaints " with monotonous regularity, and continued to slave in the factory, save for visits to the hospital on the ancient site where they saw conditions worse even than their own, and collected large bottles of medicine at the dispensary, which they stood on their machine tables and drank at intervals of the day. And the women married, and remarried, and multiplied their seed; and their children came to meet them in the evening at the factory gates.

There were exceptions to the common experience—the type. I remember Bessie, who sat at our work table and was addicted to a Society which searched the Bible for prophecies and hidden meanings, and the dates and times of impending catastrophes, the members of which were exclusive entrants to the coming millennium. The moments of every meal time Bessie gave to feverish search of the Bible, and a forelock of her hair had turned white when she was twenty-five. Her image rises familiarly before me: the exquisitely shaped hand, with its strongly delicate fingers tapering to beautiful well-kept nails, supporting her forehead as, unaware of everything about her, she pondered the pages of the Bible. And while she interested me, and I emulated the care she gave to her hands, and approved her fastidious habits and the thinly cut brown bread she brought to the factory wrapped in clean tissue paper, I was repelled by her inhuman application to the Bible, and the satisfaction she obviously got from meditating on the coming millennium, and her inclusion in this small chosen body.

Her odd employments were tolerated in that same broad, philosophical manner in which we accepted the appearance of a discoloured eye and other memorials of the conjugal felicity in the fashion. Bessie, however, did not return this expansive toleration, and I recall how she was offended into unbroken silence by our light reception of a desire she had that we should adopt, at the beginning of the New Year, a Biblical motto that should sustain us through the coming months.

Imperceptibly the novel experience of taking my place, a woman among women, began to lose its bloom. I found myself for ever dwelling on the sufferings of the women about me. I was oppressed, suffocated by them.

I cried aloud in my room at night: Then is there nothing but suffering, and misery, and ugliness without end?

It had not seemed so with Jessica and Lil. Hours I sat thinking of Jessica—and mother. Thinking in an odd, incoherent, strangely new way. Why had I not seen as now I saw? Or felt as now I felt the bitter, unpardonable injustice of their sufferings?

I thought of Mr. Mourn, and of Jessica sitting up half the night waiting for him to come home, reading the trend of events in the footsteps of people passing.

I used to like to hear that story. And did it never occur to you how Jessica *suffered?*

" Once he knocked me off the chair for sitting still and saying nothing. . . ."

I thought of mother. In new ways I thought of my mother. The dreadful wounds in her leg. Stern, set face. Not a whimper from mother; but, dear Christ! do you see mother's leg?

When first I saw it I cried, and said: " Oh mother, mother! "

Mother said: " You give me the creeps, cry-. ing. What's the good of crying? "

Mother at the wash-tub. The bad leg. Stand, stand, stand. " I want six pairs of feet and then I'd tire them all out." Mother standing on one leg. Resting the bad leg on a box. . . .

I changed—inside. I came not to know my own self. My days were consumed in rage and anger against the order of things as I saw it reflected in Jipping Street, the factory, wherever I turned my eyes. Fiercely did I range myself with the forces of the oppressed!

To such lengths was I transformed that I refused even to speak to Nellie the barmaid.

Said Nellie one day:

" Ain't you got cocky since you earned fifteen shillings a week! "

I retorted with feeling:

" I got more sense, too. You don't have to work in the factory. *You* take the money away over the bar! "

This was unpardonable rudeness to Nellie, who was always very kind to children.

I spoke impatiently to Jessica for her spirit of acquiescence towards Jipping Street, and when next she mentioned Mr. Mourn's ability to read and write I said scornfully:

" It's a pity someone didn't brain Mr. Mourn! "

My irritation exceeded all bounds, and I recall how Mrs. Bright came to Jessica's parlour that night and told us an endless story about the five children of the first Mrs. Bright, who had died not so long before. It appeared that the children of the first Mrs. Bright, bequeathed with their father to her successor, had been in the habit of eating their food off the floor.

The new mother, in an effort to introduce the

fitting and proper into a disorderly household, insisted that food should be served on a table. Cajolings and persuasions gave way to threats and blows, to be steadily repelled by the kicking and screaming of the children. It had at last occurred to the second Mrs. Bright that the panic occasioned by her well-meaning attempts was due not so much to cussedness as to sheer fear of the upright posture at meals.

In which case what was a " respectable " woman to do?

Jessica was preoccupied for days with thoughts of wooing the Bright children to more natural ways of eating, until at last I grew rude, and begged haughtily to know how she could be so absorbed in these comparatively trivial and individual matters while neglecting the larger issues of Suffering Humanity!

" What on earth does it matter," I exclaimed, " whether the Bright kids eat off the floor or at the table? "

Then Jessica looked at me, and her eyes were pained, and I was profoundly sorry for my rudeness and begged her pardon. And she said helpfully:

" Then there's the draughts to be thought of.

It can't do the kids no good sitting on the floor so much in the draughts."

It was at the time of this minor commotion that Marian Evelyn scuttled—shuffled—lurched sideways within my horizon.

She sat next to me at the work table, and because it was her abiding grief that she had been christened " Ellen Jane " instead of " Marian Evelyn " I newly christened her " Marian Evelyn."

She had got from life four children, one of whom was left to write vivid letters from America, where he had long been gone to seek his fortune; and an uncommon immunity from " complaints." Her company was made more interesting by a remarkable knowledge of trees and flowers.

She lived in a large and rather dirty house on the borders of Bermondsey, and let out her rooms to lodgers, keeping for her own home the two-roomed basement. Here she collected, with a number of stray but not unprolific cats, newspapers yellowed with age. Her genius, hardly displayed at work in the factory, was not domestic. It shone rather in her garden, a lovely place which she tended with unremitting labour.

People said that Marian Evelyn could frequently be found washing the leaves of the grass in her back garden.

There was an expression of bird-like sharpness in her face. She had a generous heart and so quaint a manner of dressing that you could not tell where her clothes began and where they ended; she looked like a round ball of unrelated garments, and she always came late to work, scuttling in with a funny, sideway lurch down the passage-way, slinking into the large room in a twinkling, taking her place at the machine with two spots of red high on her cheeks and an expression of faint surprise on her face. Among her idiosyncrasies was a reluctance to take off her clothes. She appeared to sleep fully clothed in the innumerable odds and ends of garments that ordinarily composed her dress.

Marian Evelyn was unlike anyone I had ever met, and of the bonds that linked us were our dislike of restraint, our revolutionary notions, and impatience with the factory which ate up our days. She believed in, and she supported, the Trades Union movement; but her intense feeling on this and the matter of social reform generally could find no outlet, for she was afflicted with an inarticulateness only rescued from the tragic by her acute sense of humour.

She was indeed a discovery in that arid waste of women who slaved all day and multiplied their seed and visited the hospital on the ancient site and brought back large bottles of medicine which they stood on their machine tables.

These were the days of the Suffrage agitation, and Marian Evelyn divided her scanty leisure in attendance at Suffrage meetings in the Caxton Hall and Socialist meetings in Camberwell; while the old newspapers continued to accumulate in her basement, which became less and less clean looking, and the curtains at the windows remained untouched until they fell away from their fastenings in rags and tatters.

With Marian Evelyn I, too, was fired at the Suffrage gatherings, and I remember that for many months we faithfully attended the meetings of an Ethical Society which met on Sunday evenings. Here I enriched my vocabulary, and came nearer to that correctness of speech and pronunciation that had always seemed to me both necessary and desirable.

With what transports of pride did I acquire the word " ethereal "! For days I rolled " soliloquy "

on my tongue, to the unfeigned astonishment
of Marian Evelyn, and framed questions to
the lecturer at the end of each Sunday evening
to exercise my growing ease in expression, and
the use of words that seemed beautiful to me.

Marian Evelyn could not read, and she appeared to like having me read to her some inflammatory pamphlet she had lately acquired, or
the exacerbations of Ruskin, a reprint from
Adam Smith, or Mr. Blatchford's *Merrie
England*. I eagerly embraced every opportunity
for reading aloud to practise myself in speech,
to acquire the use of unfamiliar words and exercise for my vocabulary.

Two evenings a week Marian Evelyn per-
suaded me to attend a Night School in the
Borough for the greater enrichment of my
vocabulary and more precision in speech. Here,
at the Night School, I incidentally learned the
theory of Pitman's Shorthand, for the pleasures
of the " English " class were only accessible
to those students who undertook some more
" practical " instruction. I also learned to swim,
for, in addition to practical instruction, healthy
exercise was insisted upon. I grew an acute dislike for this form of healthfulness and a little

practice saving the lives of the children in Jipping Street who frequently fell into the canal.

Many were the summer nights that Marian
Evelyn and I sat up late and talked long and
ardently in her back garden under the mulberry
tree—that is, I talked and Marian Evelyn
listened, for her inarticulateness did not leave
her even when we were only two together on a
calm summer night in her own back garden. She
was the best of listeners—sympathetic, understanding, infinitely patient, full of praise and
persuasion for others, full of a belief in their
ideas and abilities, but distressingly conscious of
her own unworthiness to contribute to the
conversation.

We discussed how hard it was to break away
from that attitude of accepted misery that encompassed us about; the excess of spirit displayed in a street fight and the tragic, soul-
deadening lack of spirit in pushing away from
Jipping Street, and the factory, and all for which
they stood.

How we fumed and fretted and raged and
swore that we would not tread the path of our
neighbours, from the dirty, sticky perambulators
with a teat stuck in the mouth to keep you quiet,

to the grave and, possibly worse than the grave, the workhouse.

For Marian Evelyn was not disheartened by her fifty odd years of age; indeed, she seemed hardly aware of them, and more than entered into the wild plans and undiscriminating ardour of my fifteen years.

Many were those long summer nights when we sought to free ourselves from the prevailing attitude of being thankful for any slavery so long as it gave us bread and a measure of security; from the tradition of measuring accomplishment and merit by the number of years one kept the same job, through sickness to death, unless one scraped together enough pounds to lend out shillings for a penny interest a week; or, being a man, opened a " book " and collected bets outside the " World On Its Toes " or at the corner of the hospital end of Jipping Street.

Solemnly we observed how curious and consistent a fact it was that if one person in Jipping Street had the least advantage in brains, initiative, or thrift, he soon turned this advantage to battening on the neighbours as a moneylender or a bookmaker. Then were the poor the worst enemies of the poor!

How different were *our* aspirations! All that we should learn, our brains, no less than our knowledge and ability, would be used in freeing our neighbours, lightening their hardships, succouring their spirits! So we talked late into the night, renewed in strength, intoxicated by the daring of our aims and intentions.

With the morning would come to me the sobering reflection that our aspirations availed us little without a plan, a purpose; that this nebulous world of a noble, altruistic poor would not be brought nearer while I continued to re-volve confusedly in my own emotions, without a known aim. And the tired faces of the women at the factory would scatter and refute my dream, and I longed for the night to come when I could sit with Marian Evelyn in her back garden, or luxuriate in the company of my books in the little white room.

Oh, then it was easy to re-mould the world!

# VII

## THE SONS AND DAUGHTERS OF REVOLT

# VII

IT was Marian Evelyn who nominated me to membership of the " Sons and Daughters of Revolt," a little company of persons who met in a back room in Camberwell. Our meetings were distinguished by a tremendous seriousness, and I am compelled to admit that the grievances we felt were worthy of something better than our windy rhetoric.

The dominating spirit of our assembly was one Jaspar, who, when he worked, was a gas-fitter's mate; and considering how infrequently he worked, it was singular how potent and fresh was the odour of gas he suffused in his presence.

He had a wide, gaunt, white face, brilliant little beady black eyes, and he affected a quiff or half-curl, so low on his forehead that it almost touched his eyebrows. He was sustained by a burning, uncompromising hatred of all who were not as poor as we were: the oppressors. The world presented no complexities to his

mind; it was made up of two classes: the oppressed and the oppressors. By violence you
withdrew from the one the means and instru-
ments of oppression, and " fed the hungry and
clothed the naked," an expression he repeated
with tedious frequency.

There trailed in the wake of Jaspar a woman
comrade of meek manners and retiring ways
and a face lamentably disfigured by some acci-
dent in childhood. She had about her a quiet
humility infinitely appealing. She never con-
tributed to the discussions, but gave freely of
her sympathetic, acquiescent presence.

In my mind she left no doubt as to her real
feelings for Jaspar, the black beady-eyed Jaspar,
who was always at much pains to example his
platonic friendship for her in his visionary and
voluble excursions to a Utopia as imminent to
him as the Second Coming to Paul and the
Millennium to Bessie in the factory.

Jaspar's rhetoric has, mercifully, faded from
my mind; the other persons of the company
assembled in the gas-lit back room in Camberwell are shadowy, fugitive memories. " Jimmy,"
with his unruly moustache and anæmic body
which yet could not hold captive his unresting

spirit, and Jimmy's large-bosomed wife who answered to the name of Flora and united to the timidity of a rabbit a habit of volcanic speech— memories these are that elude me; but I have a clear, aching memory of that still, acquiescent presence, and of hungry eyes for ever fixed on Jaspar, set in a face grotesquely maimed and disfigured. . . .

I plunged unstintingly into the feverish round of street corner meetings and back room con- ferences, and secretly wondered at the negligible results of our intemperate speech and violent intentions. I think I had little faith in our ful- minations, and as my faith continued to decrease I raged the more at street corners and worked harder in our door-to-door campaigns; and by a process of shutting my eyes to the ineffective vapourings, the too palpable absurdity of my comrades in revolt, by refusing to give way to my natural repugnance, kept up the show of my hopes and beliefs. For many weary months I gave lip service to the " Cause."

I read Marx and Mr. Blatchford, and achieved some facility in the rhetoric of the tub-thumpers, and spoke at street corners, and sedulously read the inflammatory weeklies, and was nightly intoxicated by the violence of our own words.

I felt more and more grown up. I could even laugh at Jessica's extreme innocence of the world as I began to find it. I recall with a blush into what fits of immoderate laughter I was flung when Jessica was relating to me a visit paid to Jipping Street one day by Mrs. Morgan's daughter.

Now Mrs. Morgan kept a parlour in Jipping Street full of cast-off clothing which she purchased from " ladies " who lived far away over London Bridge. Mrs. Morgan had a daughter, Florrie, who married above her station, and became herself a " lady." One day Florrie had been moved to visit her mother, and she arrived on a bicycle.

Not wishing to contaminate this vehicle from another world by too near association with the cast-off clothing, Florrie stopped outside Jessica's parlour, and sent one of the inevitable Jipping Street children to announce her arrival to her mother. Then balanced precariously, if luxuriously, against the kerb, she received Mrs. Morgan in state, to the wonder and admiration of all Jipping Street. " Such a lady! " concluded Jessica.

On reflection it troubled me that Jessica was so wanting in worldly experience, and I conceived a plan for taking her out into the world, showing her London from a larger angle than Jipping Street. I could think of nothing better than a trip to Hampton Court on one of the pleasure steamers that plied up the Thames from London Bridge.

Jessica borrowed a hat from old Mrs. Lapum, and on a Saturday in June, in a twitter of excitement, we set forth round the hospital bend, over London Bridge to the boarding stage of the " Belle o' the Thames."

We had reached Westminster when I saw that Jessica, tense and pale with distrust of the smooth waters gliding past our bows, and terrified by the dark bridges which threatened to strike us down as we approached, could bear it no longer. Feverishly clutching my arm with one hand, and the rail of the gang plank with the other, Jessica led us to the " blessed earth," turning her back with a sigh of relief on travel and adventure. Her only regret, as the jogging of the bus replaced the more subtle movements of the steamer, was for the "loverly" tickets I had bought for our journey to Hampton Court.

For weeks her remarks on this excursion into the outside world were divided between her concern for the fate of the tickets and poignant recollections of that " feeling upside down inside " which had overcome her between London Bridge and Westminster.

This adventure, however, was but an interlude stolen from more serious activities. For weeks now Marian Evelyn and I had talked of the pressing need for revolt in the factory; and at last one evening we sat down and composed a letter bringing our sweated state to the notice of a Trades Union organised for women factory workers. We pointed the letter in such tones and colours, introducing facts so poignant, that representatives of the organisation began to descend on us in sporadic visits to combine us for revolt.

After arduously canvassing the more bold spirits in the factory, we gathered together a little company that met in a parish room adjoining the local church, where in exchange for our entrance fees and the promise of a weekly subscription to the Union, we received the Union badge of membership, and bright promises of higher wages in the future.

Our company in the parish room was lamentably small, for most of the women in the factory
received with tired indifference these gentle
preachers of revolt, and were coldly sceptical of
their bright allurements for the future.

We opened our meetings with a hymn and
closed the meetings with a hymn, thus marking
our appreciation of the vicar who loaned to us
the parish room. Sometimes we were addressed
by a lady named Mrs. Sparks, who was formed
in a similarly generous mould as the violently
tongued Flora; while in the wake of Mrs. Sparks
there trailed ladies of paler texture, more softly
tongued, affecting less rough tweeds—without
the declamatory eloquence of Mrs. Sparks, made
more emphatic, as it was, by her notable lack
of breath; without her ample lines, her breeze
and decision. Her minions were also of obvious
gentility, and while one did not question the
benevolence of their intentions or the integrity
of their purpose, they impressed us chiefly with
their futility, and dismayed us by their incurably
spinster-like appearance.

If my spirit was critical about all these bright
prospects and strange persons (for I felt deeply
the sufferings of the women with whom I

worked in the factory), I gave service and collected, where I could collect, the weekly sub-
scriptions to the Union, small as they were.

Yet I could not help becoming aware of the
unreality, as it were, of our efforts to coerce a
Utopia on the strength of an extra sixpence or
two a week on our wages, in face of the bitter
reality of the conditions of the women which we
strove to alleviate; the poignancy of their
sufferings as against the rather ridiculous and
*essential* ignorance of our liberators, so kindly,
so grossly incapable of comprehending the lives
of the women they came to free.

It came to me that the women in the factory
were too tired for the revolt urged upon them,
too deeply inured to acceptance. I had no doubt
as to the utter desirableness of an increase in our
wages; I believed that this we could achieve by
the organisation advocated by the speech-makers
who came to us—if only we could have effected
the necessary organisation, unity, and flank
attacks!

Forlorn hope! For the women in the factory
continued stonily to eye the preachers of revolt,
the liberators who descended on us from unknown worlds of competence and comfort, too

palpably unblemished by the experience that was ours. Yet I do not think their insufficiency proved so great an obstacle as the subscription fees to the Trades Union from women to whom even two pennies a week represented a loaf of bread that, for a time at least, would quiet a family of hungry children.

Jessica was depressing. " You might as well try to spit in the canal long enough to make the water run over the sides," she said, and solemnly repeated the warning often on her lips : " All you'll do is get the sack." Her warning came true—in time.

One of my richest gains from these preliminary canters in rebellion was Miss Doremus, who followed in the wake of Mrs. Sparks. She was exquisitely small and frail, and her tiny face was surmounted by a great wealth of fair hair. She had the shyest of smiles, and a manner of appearing to shrink before the onslaughts of this world, coupled with a habit of self-efface-ment. Her obvious fear of us at the meetings in the parish room commended her to us; we admired, at a distance, the exquisite fragility of her form and the perfection of her clothes. She seemed positively elf-like in the shadow of the tweed-clad Miss Sparks. What she lacked in physical amplitude, however, she abundantly made up in moral courage. I have seen her fearlessly approach the burly driver of a cart-horse on Tooley Street laying about him with the whip, and quell him with her tense white face and tenser words.

She came often to my room in Jipping Street, and in the winter evenings we sat over the open flame of a gas cooking stove, our one source of heat, and pretended it was a coal fire in which we saw pictures. " Brought up very respectable, among toffs," as Jessica would say, she felt it in no way unusual that we should build a friendship over the open gas flame in Jipping Street to the sound of drunken brawls on the canal-bank, babies screaming, the Rabelaisian salutations of neighbour to neighbour, and the returning sallies of passers-by.

Miss Doremus had about her a delicacy, an allure touched with a deeply felt sympathy for all those who suffered and were in distress, which seemed to protect her even in the back streets of Bermondsey when at night she walked through to London Bridge. Her manner bore a silent apology for her privileges and advantages, and betrayed not the slightest trace of a desire to flaunt them in our faces. She came humbly to Jipping Street, not as did so many others to see how the poor lived and give them the doubtful inspiration of their presence and the even more doubtful good of their benevolence—she came humbly, and because she felt so deeply soon learned to put away any temptation she might have felt for " doing good," preferring rather to suffer with us.

With emotions of pride, I took Miss Doremus one day to see Jessica. They seemed, at first, to stand rather in awe of each other, and by this I was much confounded. Jessica twitched her shawl and sat very quiet, and constantly turned her eyes to the heavens as though she were at her devotions, being acute enough to perceive, even without the tangible evidence of a bicycle, that she was in the presence of a lady.

# VIII

# RETREAT

# VIII

Feverish, confused, baffled days, and questionings without end.

I could not but see that Jaspar was a windbag. Stick a pin in him, said Jessica, and he goes off pop. Indeed, were we not all windbags, we, the Sons and Daughters of Revolt? Except Jaspar's lady, with the maimed face, and Marian Evelyn, neither of whom opened their mouths at a back-room conference or street-corner meeting. If only they could have expressed the colour of their thoughts, the quality of their spirits. Alas! They were dumb.

Also, to complicate matters, I suffered from an extreme sensitiveness to persons. More and more did I discover in myself an inattention to their principles. I disliked Jaspar. Nay, I despised Jaspar. I could not help likening him to the fly in Æsop, who sat on the chariot wheel and cried: " My, what a dust I do raise!"

I made bold to say this. When, later, Marian Evelyn challenged me, we came to the conclusion that my irritation was due to his cavalier-like treatment of her with the grotesque face. Whereupon Marian Evelyn said that his principles were " all right," and that his platonic friendships were not our business.

I felt ashamed. When she left me I plunged into a gloomy examination of myself. I saw that, whereas I delighted in persons I liked, without regard to their political principles or even the principles of their conduct, I could not abide those whom I did not like; nor did I absolve them of personal insufficiency on the possession of excellent principles.

From gloom I sank to further gloom, and I have no doubt that my meditations took the colour of an incident which had occurred early in the evening at a meeting of the Sons and Daughters of Revolt.

The extreme views of our company included what was called " Atheism ": Ingersoll and Bradlaugh supplied the text. We were this night considering the subject of hell in its uses to the capitalist through the clergy and priesthood. I was rash enough to contribute uninvited to the

discussion, my enthusiasm betraying me into
irrelevancies and a prolix utterance.

For my encounters with hell as a child had
been rather triumphant; and they were oddly
mixed up with a belief that " God is Love." I
believed in love—in a large, impersonal love; and
it pleased me often to remember that " God is
Love," a text much distributed among the poor,
the significance of which came to me one day
when I was battling with the hell of blood and
thunder promised to all unbelievers in the
Mission Hall, and at the top of Jipping Street
where the Salvation Army gathered every Sunday and played a brass band before calling on
heaven to witness our extreme need and un-
repentance.

The thought of hell took vivid and violent
hold on my imagination, and for a long time I
shrank from the demon in prospect. Then one
day it occurred to me with the suddenness of an
inspiration that, if God was Love, then indeed
he must be like Jessica, who would not hurt the
meanest creature, and found forgiveness and
understanding for everyone.

I long meditated on this analogy, and ulti-
mately it brought me an ecstasy of release from

the oppression of hell as it was painted in the
Mission Hall and confirmed every Sunday by
the Salvation Army at the top of Jipping Street.

So it was that with me hell early lost its sting,
I said in my peroration. Vaguely, nebulously, in
the back of my mind, I held the comforting
thought of love—and God—in the person of
Jessica, who profoundly believes in " Them
what's above."

Flushed, and a little bothered, I sat down, and
my testimony was greeted with cries of derision,
led by Jaspar, who said, assuming a curate-like
air, and being transported to irrelevancies even
more absurd than my own: " Pray now, brothers
and sisters, let us love the Capitalist . . ." and
much else that I have forgotten. I, however, can
never forget the agony of embarrassment I
suffered for what Jaspar was pleased to call my
" hoity-toity " turn of mind, although in my
heart I did not believe that I was " hoity-
toity."

I thought of Jessica and her exceeding compassion; of her faith in " Them what's above ";
and now it seemed that when I thought of
Jessica, Jaspar and all our company of Revolt
assumed less glowing colours. I recalled my

excursions with her only a few days before to the sick bed of Poppy Lapum's sister Lizzie, who had long been hovering at death's door. And old Mrs. Lapum, her mother, was beside herself with grief, for Lizzie, in addition to being a " good girl," was her main support.

One day when Lizzie was said to have reached an extremity of suffering, and feeling ran high in Jipping Street against Mrs. Lapum for refusing to summon the beneficences of the local clergyman to Lizzie's aid, Jessica, notwithstanding Mrs. Lapum's reputation for contumely, accosted her outside the " World On Its Toes."

" Why don't you 'ave the clergyman in to say a few prayers for Lizzie?" Jessica said, more in pain than in rebuke. " It won't do no 'arm and it might do some good."

" I don't want no clergyman in my 'ouse," said Mrs. Lapum fiercely.

" Well, don't be an 'eathen," said Jessica gently. " I'll come myself, if you'll let me. I only know the Lord's Prayer, but Lizzie's welcome to that."

We went in the evening to Lizzie's bedside. Jessica sat down by the bed while I, dismayed, and a little frightened at Lizzie's look of exhaustion, withdrew to the doorway, where, behind old Mrs. Lapum, I watched Jessica smooth Lizzie's hair and croon her words of comfort, which brought a smile to Lizzie's face; and we closed our eyes when Jessica said the Lord's Prayer.

Lizzie appeared to be much comforted, and old Mrs. Lapum dissolved into quiet weeping, and when we bade her good night at the door Jessica said again: " All I ses is, it don't do no 'arm, and it might do some good."

From melancholy I passed to even more melancholy thought; and I saw that my days were troubled with an unrest that I could not shape and which found little ease in the company of the Sons and Daughters of Revolt, or in stirring up trouble at the factory for the benefit of the Union and a doubtful increase some day in our wages. Moreover, I could not resign myself to a life of hideous work in the factory, rounded out by death and possibly the workhouse. This and other small tragedies exercised my soul.

I found myself becoming more anxious about Jessica. She looked paler than usual, she appeared to be more tired, and notwithstanding that Nellie the barmaid said that Jessica looked more and more as if she " ware all going to pieces," I could not be certain whether she was, in fact, becoming ill, or whether I was disturbed by the possibility of a widening of the breach between us.

I retired more to my little room—my citadel; reward of my imposture at the factory in those first, harassed days. It made possible the days which did not belong to me. Always there was the early morning which was mine; mine, too, were the late hours of the night alone in my room. *There* were no worn faces to scatter my dreams. I could draw the curtains and shut out the ugliness and squalor and the light of day. Oh, I could not bear the light of day, for in it everything seemed more hopeless and unlovely! The night is more kindly.

I had stripped the walls of their dirty and verminous paper, and with a liberal use of whitewash brought them nearer to the clean white walls of my heart's delight. Other nights I scrubbed the floor, and it, too, shone white and clean. I could not mend the windows, but I covered the cracks with brown paper, which I pasted to the frame. I owned one chair without a back, but with a surface washed as clean and white as the floor and the walls, and on this I sat, night after night, and looked at my books on the mantelpiece, and set out, in my mind's eye, the bookshelves I should one day build me round the strong deal table I should one day buy; but for the time I was more than happy to breathe in the solitude and feast my eyes on the white walls and clean fresh floor-boards.

My room was like a world apart, and every night and every morning I was re-created in its solitude, girded, armoured for the day before me, and the people, whose very presence laughed at my secret thoughts.

My library grew and increased, and I assiduously cultivated the lady at the Mission Hall, who gave me Emerson and the *Road-mender*, the *Imitation* and a Bible issued from the Oxford Press, whose illustrations I tore out as they offended me, and whose other contents I devoured with a pleasure not put off by early religious instruction.

Miss Le Grand, when she died in the workhouse, left her library with Jessica, who at once bequeathed it to me; so that with my *Road-*

*mender* and the *Imitation* now stood *Sonnets from the Portuguese*, a mutilated edition of Isaac Disraeli's *Curiosities of Literature*, a positively greasy-looking copy of Percy's *Reliques*, a prayer-book for use in the *Church of England*, and one volume of Montaigne, which I did not often read, for the wise scepticism of the illustrious Frenchman sorted ill with my strivings at this time.

I had bought myself the *Decline and Fall* and Macaulay's *History of England*, so soon as I had paid for my curtains and the couch in my room on which I slept. These histories I devoured from beginning to end, and again from beginning to end clandestinely, in the factory, with one eye on my work and the other eye on the book. I have a particular reason for remembering at least one part of Gibbon, the outline of Christianity, in its beginnings, which comes in an early part of the second volume. It was at this part that I put the first finger of my left hand under the needle of the machine, instead of a collar. I have to-day the honourable scar and an ineffaceable memory of one or two facts —after Gibbon—concerning the beginnings of Christianity.

I derived great pleasure from these histories, which, as I grew up, I heard slighted, maligned. The colour and movement of Macaulay, the onward swing from Parliament to Parliament and from King to King, daily transported me, nor was my pleasure spoiled by any awareness of his prejudices or inaccuracies.

From the Nelson Library I purchased for sevenpence Macaulay's *Literary Essays* on Fanny Burney, Bacon, Leigh Hunt and John Bunyan. Books about books I found even more entrancing than histories.

I recall at this time buying Gibbon's Autobiography, and if I found it less fascinating than the *Decline and Fall*, I none the less read it with much relish. The historian's encounter with Mademoiselle Suzanne Curchod I especially delighted in: its brief and chequered course, its climax with Gibbon the elder's repudiation of the proposed marriage.

" I yielded to my fate; I sighed as a lover; I obeyed as a son; my wound was insensibly healed by time, absence, and the habits of a new life. My cure was accelerated by a faithful report of the tranquillity and cheerfulness of the lady, and my love subsided to friendship and esteem."

This I thought exquisitely funny, and I well remember it, for the awe and reverence it was my habit to bring to my reading seldom permitted me to perceive anything funny. No devotee approached the symbol of his faith more devoutly, more humbly than did I approach the glories of our language as they then appeared to me.

I confess that the *sense* of these books was often uncomprehended by me—only the *sound* was not lost—and there was nothing that brought sweeter music to my soul than the sound of beautiful words. The Blessing, for example, in the Communion Service: " The peace of God, which passeth all understanding, keep your hearts and minds in the knowledge and love of God, and of his Son Jesus Christ our Lord: and the blessing of God Almighty, the Father, the Son, and the Holy Ghost, be amongst you and remain with you always."

I knew it by heart. I read it aloud in my room at night. I repeated it to myself in the factory where I alone could hear myself speak, for the noise of the machinery was so great.

I read the *Sonnets from the Portuguese*—I learned them by heart, many of them. I read the

*Imitation* before I went to bed at night. Oh, sweet and savoury words, to the sound of which I so often went to sleep! and if its exhortations to holiness and a contrite heart fell on indifferent soil, I was humbled by the lovely simplicity of its words.

With Gibbon I hesitate, from the apprehension of ridicule, before laying bare the category into which my reading unconsciously fell. I could not go to sleep at night either to the melodies of *Twelfth Night* or the sheer poetry of the *Ode to a Nightingale*. My need was for less subtle consolations, and my need was great. Hence my addiction to Emerson, that bucolic optimist, with his infinitely obvious appeal to Courage and Self-reliance, his Compensation.

Much did I owe to the Transcendentalist of Concord in those days when I came to read less and less of the revolutionary literature that had absorbed my spare time in the early days at the factory. Each morning I set out for the factory with some fresh phrase from Emerson to whip my flagging spirits, to fix my thought on things above!

What to do, however? Whither to aspire? If only there were not Jipping Street, and the factory, and mother; and I could read all day and set down my dreams!

Life then was like walking on a parapet, looking neither to the right nor to the left, looking straight ahead, pressing on and on, encompassed about with fears, nameless fears; shutting out but not forgetting.

There remained, however, my room—my citadel. Oh the inexpressible balm of its bareness! No odds and ends; no cheap china pieces with inflexible countenances; nor photographs, nor stuffed chairs smelling with age and the need for fresh air—none of those things which made up the real Gethsemane of my childhood. Only the line of the room (small though it was); my books now on shelves made from those excellent Tate sugar-boxes and stained to resemble oak; clean-smelling, fresh white-washed walls; and I no longer looked up at my grandfather's memorial card on which, with the date of his death, was inscribed the fact that his body was washed up at Mortlake.

Blue curtains at the windows matching the blue covering of the couch—a deep, rich, unfathomable blue.

My landlady, the moneylender, shivered as

139

with the cold when she beheld the bareness of my room. She said acidly, " You might as well be in an 'ospital," and retired hastily to the swarming knick-knacks in her parlour, where, under a picture of the Crucifixion, depicted in a manner unsparing of physical detail, she received her clients when they came to borrow sixpence or a shilling.

# IX

# THE PASSING OF JESSICA MOURN

# I X

FOR a long time now Jessica had been sickening
of an illness that first came to her in stretches
of great tiredness, of flutterings about the heart.
She took to her couch frequently, and the dust
began to accumulate on the vase of dyed grass
that had belonged to her mother; the white
apron took on a forlorn air, a limpness; and her
parlour in Jipping Street, so neat and clean,
came to look a little blown upon and tired, like
Jessica. These and other symptoms we noted
with growing concern.

We saw her no longer at her door, wrapped
in the black shawl and an aura of deep quiet that
rebuked the unresting street, and for more weeks
than we cared to remember we saw no rim of
white hearthstone on the pavement immediately
outside her front door, which served to create
the illusion of a step to the house—a tradition
borrowed from her mother and the days of Kent
Street.

As she came the more to shrink in her shawl, now hardly rising from the couch all day, we were thrown into the utmost dismay, and begged of her to see a doctor; but this she would not consider. Nor could we coax or persuade her to the hospital on the ancient site. She abhorred the place since Maggie Murphy went in to be cut about the ear, and, getting mixed up with the tonsil cases, came out without her tonsils.

I spent my early mornings with Jessica and the hours of the evening. There were nights when I slept in the parlour, conscious of a new fear that she might slip away, unknown to us. And if I could not entertain the thought of losing Jessica, or believe that it was possible, her quiet, insistent assurance that her days were numbered made me obedient to her least desire. I humoured her; I met her every wish.

I made a pilgrimage over London Bridge to the head office of the Insurance Company to whom she paid two pennies a week for her last " turn-out "—a hearse, and one coach to follow for the mourners. I brought back to the parlour assurance that her affairs were in good order and that she would be " going decent," as Jessica felt one should go. Then, before she seemed to lose touch with the Present and Jipping Street, I, for the last time, pledged my honour I would see that her feet were clean when they came to lay her out.

For Jessica had a peculiar sensitiveness on the subject of her feet, and in times of despondency often declared that she knew she would be found in her last hour with feet a trifle dirty. This was repugnant to her delicate soul. She said that if she washed her feet one day they would be, the next day, as dusty as if she had never washed them. She attributed this to the spring-side boots she wore, which admitted the dust into their sides and the dye from her stockings.

Slow-moving days, heavy with sadness; we seemed to live in an unchanging twilight. Jessica had lost awareness of the Present and the life about her; her hold on Jipping Street, ever tenuous, seemed now utterly to relax.

She would sleep a fitful sleep, and wake and call me and ask feverishly if the brushes were finished; as if she were again in the basement sitting at the bench, listening to her mother's stories, with the world walking overhead, rattling the gratings as it passed down Kent Street. I would endeavour to chide her playfully for

145

mixing us all up with the basement and the brushes.

Nights there were, unending nights—when the smell of the chloroform from the hospital on the ancient site seemed to have drugged the unfeeling world to sleep—and she would seem to gather together her fading strength and ask me to read. The flicker of a twinkle in her eyes, a softening of the set lines that pain brings to the face, and I would raise the pillow on which her head rested, and read to her from Old Moore's Almanack, for Jessica was fond of the Almanack.

I endeavoured to tell her stories to pass the long hours, and vary the monotony of Old Moore's Almanack, which moved with leaden pace from the foretelling of floods and disasters to the deaths of kings and princes. The consciousness of my imperfections as a story-teller to one who had listened, as Jessica had listened, to the stories her mother re-created from the novelettes greatly hampered my endeavours.

Now as I returned to her at night it seemed to me that she lay ever between sleeping and waking. There were fleeting intervals when she spoke of Dr. Acton: " Our Lord's footsteps over again "; coming back always to the basement and the days of Kent Street, when you had only to *look* hungrily in the pie and pudding shop to get two-pennyworth of currant duff for a ha'penny.

With little experience of illness, and in spite of a wilful blindness to the evidences of her grave condition, I knew at last that Jessica must have a doctor. Yet I could not bring myself ruthlessly to violate her express command, to rouse the antagonism of the stubborn, if gentle, will that looked at me out of brown eyes. I therefore introduced the doctor in the guise of a caller from the Insurance Company.

The doctor could do little but prescribe a drug to lessen the pain. To me his visit was hardly reassuring, and Jessica, in spite of the disguise, looked upon it with suspicion.

She received more cordially Mr. Mumford from the Mission Hall, who came to give occasional comfort from the Bible, for Jessica had always felt that, as with a few prayers, a verse or two from the Bible " can't do no 'arm and might do some good."

Her thoughts were often with " Them what's above," and as she slowly passed beyond the long reach of pain there came to her face a

147

great calm. From time to time I was reminded of her hope, seldom, if earnestly, expressed, of "having a few words with Jesus' Mother, for being a woman she must understand."

Then at last she opened her large brown eyes full on me, and I saw not pity nor compassion, nor pain nor hurt, for Jessica had gone away.

In the moment of stillness that followed I heard a voice crying—

"And Christ slept, and His saints."

# X

# WHITHER?

# X

MOTHER would say I must shut my mouth and
go on, and if I do not find in myself her fine
flinty endurance, her fearlessness, that granite-
like quality against which joy and grief are alike
impotent, I am not wholly without courage.

The bonds that held me to Jipping Street are
loosening; familiar things in my childhood have
lost their meaning or, like Jessica and Lil, have
gone away. Within me, ever more clear and insistent, is the urge that knows no rest; but
whither? to what end?

I must talk with someone. Mother would only
laugh—" Life kicks you downstairs and then it
kicks you upstairs "—but I know that there is
more. I cannot shape this knowledge even to
myself; but in my books, in beautiful words,
there is something strangely like my dreams:
they smile on me, beckon to me.

I must go on, following without seeing where
they lead.

If you would like to know more about Virago books, write to us at Ely House, 37 Dover Street, London W1X 4HS for a full catalogue.

*Please send a stamped addressed envelope*

### VIRAGO
*Advisory Group*

**Book Tokens**

**Give them the pleasure of choosing**
Book Tokens can be bought and exchanged at most bookshops.